Coaching Principles
Workbook

FOURTH EDITION

American Sport
Education Program

Human Kinetics

ISBN-10: 1-4504-1297-1 (print)
ISBN-13: 978-1-4504-1297-1 (print)

Acquisitions Editor: James Schmutz
Managing Editors: Coree Clark and Amy Stahl
Assistant Editors: Derek Campbell and Elizabeth Evans
Copyeditor: Amanda M. Eastin-Allen
Graphic Designer: Nancy Rasmus
Graphic Artist: Tara Welsch
Cover Designer: Keith Blomberg
Printer: United Graphics

Printed in the United States of America   10 9 8 7 6 5 4 3 2 1

The paper in this book is certified under a sustainable forestry program.

Human Kinetics
Website: www.HumanKinetics.com

United States: Human Kinetics
P.O. Box 5076
Champaign, IL 61825-5076
800-747-4457
e-mail: humank@hkusa.com

Canada: Human Kinetics
475 Devonshire Road Unit 100
Windsor, ON N8Y 2L5
800-465-7301 (in Canada only)
e-mail: info@hkcanada.com

Europe: Human Kinetics
107 Bradford Road
Stanningley
Leeds LS28 6AT, United Kingdom
+44 (0) 113 255 5665
e-mail: hk@hkeurope.com

Australia: Human Kinetics
57A Price Avenue
Lower Mitcham, South Australia 5062
08 8372 0999
e-mail: info@hkaustralia.com

New Zealand: Human Kinetics
P.O. Box 80
Torrens Park, South Australia 5062
0800 222 062
e-mail: info@hknewzealand.com

E5507

CONTENTS

PREFACE

Welcome to the Coaching Principles course! The goal of this course is to help you become the most successful coach that you can be. The classroom course, test preparation, and Coaching Successfully activities will help you develop your coaching philosophy, motivate your athletes, teach techniques and tactics, develop training programs, plan for the season and each practice, and manage your team and your relationships with all of the people you work with.

Coaching Principles Workbook is your guide and resource for completing the three activities mentioned previously: classroom course, test preparation, and Coaching Successfully activities. You'll use it during the classroom course as your instructor leads you through activities, videos, and discussions. All of the resources you need for the classroom course are in the workbook, and plenty of space has been left for you to write notes.

After you've completed the classroom course, you'll use the test preparation assignments included at the end of classroom units 2 through 7 to prepare for the Coaching Principles test. These assignments include reading the course text, *Successful Coaching*, and working through the units in *Coaching Principles Online* component. Attending the classroom course, reading the text, and completing the online component should prepare you for the Coaching Principles test. Just as important, these activities should enhance your likelihood of becoming a successful coach.

ASEP hopes that you find the course and supporting resources valuable in contributing to your efforts to be a successful coach. We wish you the best of success in providing meaningful sport experiences for your athletes.

Introduction to Coaching Principles

PURPOSE To examine why you want to coach and to introduce the Coaching Principles course, including the course resources, purpose, learning objectives, agenda, and test preparation and test procedures.

Learning Objectives

In this unit you will learn about

- some of the reasons you have for coaching;
- course resources;
- purpose, learning objectives, and agenda for Coaching Principles; and
- procedures for completing the test preparation and test phases of the course.

UNIT OVERVIEW

Topic	Activities	Time (min)
A. Welcome	Course welcome Course resources	10
B. Why You're Here	Section introduction Activity 1.1 Why Coaching?	15
C. Introduction to Coaching Principles	Section introduction DVD 1 Introduction to Coaching Principles	5
D. Completing the Course	Section introduction Purpose, objectives, and agenda for the course Procedures for completing the test preparation and test phases of the course Housekeeping details Unit summary	10
TOTAL MINUTES		**40**

Welcome

(Notes)

Course Packages

- The course text, *Successful Coaching,* or, alternatively, a key code letter (included in the test package) with the key code to access the *Successful Coaching* e-book
- *Coaching Principles Workbook*
- The Coaching Principles classroom test package, including the following:
  - Coaching Principles classroom test
  - ASEP Test Answer Form A to record test answers
  - Coaching Principles test instructions
  - Preaddressed ASEP mailing envelope for the coach to use for mailing the completed ASEP Test Answer Form A
  - Cardboard insert to ensure that the test form is not damaged in the mail
  - Key code letter with the key code to access *Coaching Principles Online* component

Coaching Principles Workbook

- Each unit includes the following:
  - Unit's purpose, learning objectives, overview, and sections (A, B, and so forth)
  - Summary of the unit introduction
  - For every activity: an introduction; instructions that describe the resources to use, steps to complete, and the outcome of your work; and activity worksheets for you to write on to complete the activity
  - In the workbook: space for you to write notes (for example, during section introductions and DVDs). This space is denoted with the word "notes" in parentheses.
  - Test preparation activities that you should complete on your own after today to prepare for the test (note: unit 1 does not have test preparation activities)
  - Coaching Successfully activities, which you'll complete after the test (note: unit 1 does not have Coaching Successfully activities)

Successful Coaching

- Five parts: Principles of Coaching, Principles of Behavior, Principles of Teaching, Principles of Physical Training, and Principles of Management

- Latest sport science research, practical knowledge acquired by highly experienced coaches, and references from leading experts
- Illustrations, photos, tables, and forms

Test Options

- You can complete the course test using a paper–pencil form, or you can complete it online.
- Everything you'll need to do for either test is described in the Coaching Principles test instructions booklet.

Test Information

- If you take the paper–pencil test, you'll enter this information on the answer form.
- If you take the online test, you'll enter this information online.

REFER to the Test Information form on page 105 in *Coaching Principles Workbook,* and **ENTER** the information described by the instructor.

B. Why You're Here

(Notes)

Activity 1.1 Why Coaching?

Instructions

1. Work individually.
2. In the space provided, list the three most important reasons you have for wanting to coach.
3. Number your reasons by importance, using 1 for most important, 2 for less important, and 3 for least important.
4. You'll have two minutes to complete your list.
5. After you've completed your list, you'll introduce yourself and share your list with the class.

Reasons for wanting to coach:

Introduction
- Name
- Present position
- Sports coached
- Length of career
- Top three reasons to coach

C. Introduction to Coaching Principles

(Notes)

DVD 1 Introduction to Coaching Principles

(Notes)

D. Completing the Course

(Notes)

Coaching Principles Classroom Course Agenda

Unit number	Unit title	Time (min)
1	Introduction to Coaching Principles	40
2	Principles of Coaching	85
	Break	10
3	Principles of Management	65
4	Principles of Physical Training	30
	Lunch	45
5	Principles of Behavior	95
	Break	10
6	Principles of Teaching	140
7	Coaching Principles Wrap-Up	15
	Total minutes (units only)	**470**

Course Topics

- This morning, we'll discuss the principles of coaching, the principles of management, and the principles of physical training.
    - You'll consider and start to define what matters to you as a coach.
    - We'll discuss different coaching styles, and you'll consider which style or combination of styles you want to use in your coaching career.
    - We'll discuss some of the key people you'll interact with as a coach, including parents, other coaches, administrators, and officials.
    - You'll learn about your legal duties as a coach and about your responsibility to help manage the risks involved with making the athletes' participation as safe as possible.
    - You'll consider how to manage your time to accomplish all you must do.
    - We'll discuss what you need to know in order to ensure the physical preparation of your athletes, including proper nutrition and addressing and preventing illegal drug use.
- We'll have a midmorning break and a break for lunch.
- This afternoon we'll discuss the principles of behavior, take a break, and then discuss the principles of teaching.
    - We'll discuss how to engage and encourage athletes, including the keys to communicating with and managing your relationships with them.
    - You'll learn how to use motivation and discipline to coach responsibly and to create an environment in which athletes can have fun and feel worthy.
    - You'll consider things to do and not do in order to create an environment of respect for your program and for all types of athletes.
    - You'll learn how to teach the technical and tactical skills of your sport and to evaluate and provide feedback for your athletes' learning and performance.
    - We'll discuss techniques for developing your athletes' attention, concentration, and decision-making skills.
    - You'll learn how to use the games and traditional approaches to teaching.
    - You'll learn how to create a season plan and how to plan challenging practices.
- Before you head home, we'll wrap things up and discuss how you can use *Successful Coaching,* the workbook, and *Coaching Principles Online* component to prepare for the Coaching Principles classroom test.

Test Preparation and Test Procedures

- Over the next several weeks, you need to complete the other phases of Coaching Principles—the test preparation phase of the course and the Coaching Principles test.
  - The steps for completing the test are described in the Coaching Principles test instructions included in your test package.
  - You should plan to complete these activities by _____.
  - If you do not pass your Coaching Principles test within one year of the last date of your course (today), you will have to take the entire course over again and pay all of the course fees again.
- Before you take the test, you should read *Successful Coaching* and complete the related test preparation activities listed in the workbook at the end of units 2 through 6.
  - The activities are organized by the chapters in *Successful Coaching.*
  - Some of the test preparation activities are from *Coaching Principles Online* component, and you'll complete these activities online. Instructions for accessing the online activities are included in the key code letter in your course package.
  - All of the activities we complete today and all of the activities you complete during the test preparation will help you become an effective coach and will help you pass the test. However, **do not fail to carefully read** every chapter in *Successful Coaching* because all of the test questions are based on content in the book.
- The last thing you'll do to complete the course is complete the course test.
  - You can complete the paper–pencil test, or you can complete the test online.
  - The instructions and forms you'll need to complete the course test are included in this Coaching Principles classroom test package.
  - The package contains the Coaching Principles test instructions, which provide a detailed description of what you need to do to complete the course test. After reading *Successful Coaching* and completing the related activities, you really have only three things to do:
    1. Decide whether you'll complete the test paper–pencil or online.
    2. Complete the test.
    3. Get your test scored.

- At the end of the course today, we'll discuss things you should consider in deciding whether to take the paper–pencil test or the online test.
- Whichever test you take, it's important to remember the following:
  - The course test is open book. You can refer to *Successful Coaching* and any other course materials while you complete the test.
  - You should complete the test individually unless the instructor tells you otherwise.
  - If you do not pass the test the first time, you can take it again. The procedures for taking a retest are described in the test instructions.
  - If you complete your first test paper–pencil, you must complete retests in the paper–pencil format. If you complete your first test online, you must complete retests in the online format.

E. Unit Summary

(Notes)

Principles of Coaching

PURPOSE To help you define your coaching philosophy and determine what is important to you as a coach, and to examine your coaching style.

Learning Objectives

In this unit you will learn about

- the importance of defining your coaching philosophy and what is important to you as a coach, and
- coaching styles and how they affect coaching effectiveness.

UNIT OVERVIEW

Topic	Activities	Time (min)
A. Unit Introduction	Unit introduction	5
B. Defining Your Coaching Philosophy	Section introduction Activity 2.1 Making the Tough Call With Good Decisions DVD 2 Athletes First, Winning Second Activity 2.2 Athletes First, Winning Second Activity 2.3 Coaching Successfully	50
C. Examining Coaching Styles	Section introduction Activity 2.4, Part 1 Your Favorite Coach DVD 3 Styles of Successful Coaches Activity 2.4, Part 2 Your Favorite Coach	25
D. Unit Summary	Unit summary Test preparation Coaching Successfully tips Coaching Successfully notes	5
TOTAL MINUTES		**85**

A. Unit Introduction

In unit 2 we'll discuss the principles of coaching, starting with this one: the best coaches use an athlete-centered approach that emphasizes developing young people into responsible, respectful, and disciplined student-athletes. To help you understand what this means, this unit includes the following sections.

- Defining Your Coaching Philosophy starts with an activity that illustrates how your decisions reflect what is important to you as a coach, to the athletes and their parents, and to the program and its administrators. It also illustrates why it is important for you to plan and prepare to make these decisions before they happen.
  - Then, in a DVD and a related activity, you'll consider the importance of making "Athletes first, winning second" decisions.
  - Finally, in a third activity, you'll rate the importance you place on 12 goals for developing coaches. You'll add notes about these goals throughout the rest of the course.
- Examining Coaching Styles begins with a discussion about your favorite coaches and the styles that made them successful.
  - Then, in a DVD, you'll learn more about the styles of successful coaches.
  - Finally, we'll compare the styles of your favorite coaches with the styles discussed in the DVD.
- When we've completed this unit, you should be able to
  - explain the importance of defining your coaching philosophy and determining what is important to you as a coach, and
  - describe styles of coaching and how they affect coaching effectiveness.

B. Defining Your Coaching Philosophy

(Notes)

Activity 2.1 Making the Tough Call With Good Decisions

Instructions

1. Use the No Dilemma on Discipline scenario that follows these instructions.
2. Work in teams.
3. Select a spokesperson to take notes and present the team's answers to the class.
4. Read the scenario, and discuss and answer the questions posed.
5. You'll have about 10 minutes for this activity.
6. When you're done, you should have read the scenario and answered two questions about making good decisions.

No Dilemma on Discipline

Coach Mitchell's football team, the Wildcats, is down 14 to 10 with one minute to play. The fans scream as Recordbook Rodney, the star tailback, spins away from two tackles, dodges another, and then lunges forward, tackled six yards short of the end zone. Cheering teammates surround Rodney, who—unseen by the officials—takes a cheap shot to the kidney of his tackler. When Rodney gets to his feet, he spits toward the tackler, who is in obvious pain, and then glances to the sidelines to find Coach Mitchell's eyes fixed on him. Unfortunately, the coach has seen this kind of behavior from Rodney before.

The officials call in the chains while the other team's trainer assists the injured tackler. The crowd roars as the signal is given: first down and goal. Coach Mitchell calls a time-out. Several players slap Rodney on the back as they run to the sidelines, and the PA system announces, "This is it, Wildcat fans! Six yards away from the first playoff season in 15 years of Huntsville football."

Think about the incredible amount of pressure that Coach Mitchell is under, not only due to the tense game situation but also because his best player has just conducted himself in an injurious, unsportsmanlike manner. Now, during the time-out, Coach Mitchell must make a critical decision that will likely affect the outcome of the game, Rodney, the team, and his coaching career.

1. What should Coach Mitchell do?

2. Assume that Coach Mitchell removed Rodney from the game and answer the following questions.

   a. What principles should motivate and guide Coach Mitchell's decision?

   b. What are the implications of Coach Mitchell's actions?

Activity 2.1 Making the Tough Call With Good Decisions—SAMPLE SOLUTION

1. What should Coach Mitchell do?

Response: Unfortunately, by his actions, Rodney has dictated his removal from the game. Such behavior simply can't be tolerated regardless of the game situation. Given that this is not Rodney's first transgression of this type, Coach Mitchell has almost certainly forewarned him of the consequences (including automatic removal from competition and potential suspension for games or the season). Removing Rodney from the game is merely consistent with the penalties previously explained to him.

Consider these coaching points:

The decision to remove Rodney is independent of any consideration about winning or losing the game. Coach Mitchell wanted to ensure that Rodney's emotions did not detract further from the team. He would have been wise to have an assistant coach take Rodney aside and calm him down so that no additional, emotionally driven misdeeds occur.

Refocus quickly on the game, the appropriate substitution for Rodney, and the next play. The sooner you turn your attention to the players that are available and the tactics most likely to produce a winning score, the less the impact Rodney's removal will have on the rest of the team.

If you established rules of conduct from day one with your players and have taken every disciplinary measure in a manner that is consistent with those guidelines, no player on the team (except, perhaps, Rodney) will question the decision.

In such a situation, you would need to be prepared to have one of your assistant coaches take Rodney aside and defuse him. Rodney may react on the sideline in a way that will make a bad situation a disaster for him, the team, and yourself. Head coaches need to coach their assistant coaches to be buffers in certain situations.

2. Assume that Coach Mitchell removed Rodney from the game and answer the following questions.

   a. What principles should motivate and guide Coach Mitchell's decision?

   Upholding the high standards for behavior that he defined for the team at the beginning of the season.

   Integrity of the program and principles of respectful behavior take precedence over winning.

b. What are the implications of Coach Mitchell's actions?

Some players and parents may disagree with the decision until their emotions ebb and they can put things into proper perspective.

Players will realize that, in the long run, the team benefits if selfish and dirty behavior is not tolerated.

Parents, too, will recognize the rewards of having their children in a program that will not sacrifice standards of conduct for points on the scoreboard.

A stained playoff berth is hardly worth the program's loss of respect. By staying true to the sound core values guiding his coaching philosophy, Coach Mitchell provides a good example for all his athletes and his peers.

DVD 2 Athletes First, Winning Second

(Notes)

Activity 2.2 Athletes First, Winning Second

Instructions

1. Use the Athletes First, Winning Second scenarios that follow these instructions.
2. Work individually.
3. Read the scenarios and answer the questions.
4. You'll have five minutes for this activity.
5. When you're done, you should have answered three questions and be prepared to share your answers with the class.

Scenario 1: Playing Time

Fall camp is coming to a close and John, your senior quarterback, comes into your office with a problem after practice. John is a great kid and has become the leader of your team. He's been your starting quarterback for the past two seasons and has been selected as a team captain for the second straight year by his teammates. Over the summer, a transfer quarterback moved into your district, and he's winning the position from John. John is obviously disappointed. He knows that the backup quarterback gets very little playing time over the course of a season, and he wants to quit the team.

1. What would you do? How would you respond to John? If you'd respond differently from the choices that follow, describe your response in the space provided.

   a. Tell John that you understand why quitting might be an understandable initial response, but that you don't believe he's a quitter. Ask him to think it over for a day or two. If at that point he still feels that he would not be happy as the backup quarterback, thank him for all he has done for your program and wish him well.

   b. Tell John that football is a team game and that this is varsity football and the best players play. He needs to accept his role as the backup quarterback and should keep in mind how frequently second stringers—due to starters' injuries or subpar performance—get a chance to impact a game and season.

   c. Tell John that although he won't start at quarterback, he can play a critical role on the team. Ask him to consider trying another position that suits his abilities and fills the team's needs. Note that though he won't be taking snaps from center he's still considered to be a leader by his peers, and that by embracing another role on the team he will strengthen that perception and the quality of the team.

   d. Explain to John that his leadership role on the team doesn't depend on his status as a starter. He is critical to the team's success. Tell John that how he responds to this situation will speak volumes about his character and how he will learn to face difficult situations in the future. Ask John to accept the backup role and to become a mentor coach for the transfer quarterback and his teammates.

   e. (add your response)

Scenario 2: Problem Parent

Fred is a former baseball player who bounced around the minor leagues for a few years and is now living in your district. His daughter Sue is a member of your softball team. Fred is continually complaining about your game tactics and the way you're teaching Sue how to hit. He is very vocal in the stands at your games and has started attending your practices. He's becoming a real nuisance, and his actions are having a negative effect on Sue's attitude and performance. Sue's teammates are beginning to make fun of her because of her dad. Something must be done before Fred's actions wreck the entire season.

1. What would you do? If you'd respond differently from the choices that follow, describe your response in the space provided.

   a. Confront Fred in private and tell him that his comments are not welcome. Tell him that if he keeps it up, you're going to kick his daughter off of the team.

> continued

b. Wait for the right moment during a game when Fred is mouthing off and call a time-out. Ask your athletic director to remove Fred from the school property, and ban him from the rest of your games. Make sure everyone in the stands hears your request!

c. Ask Fred if he's interested in becoming an assistant coach.

d. Call Fred at home and ask him for a private meeting in your office. Ask your athletic director to attend the meeting. When Fred arrives, thank him for coming and ask him about his playing career. Explain that you are concerned about Sue. She is losing her confidence and seems to be depressed most of the time. Tell Fred that you believe his comments and actions are having a negative effect on Sue and that you want to work things out to solve the problem. Let Fred know that your first concern is the well-being of his daughter.

e. (add your response)

Scenario 3: Hot Head

Kandace, one of your starters, has a problem with authority. She's a good player but constantly complains about calls made by the officials, even when they're obviously correct. In overtime against your league rival, Tamika drives for the basket and is stripped of the ball by an opposing player. The official does not call a foul, and Kandace instantly begins complaining. The official on the other side of the court runs into the play and calls a foul on the defender. Kandace mouths off to the first official and begins beating her chest and is immediately hit with a technical foul.

1. What would you do? If you'd respond differently from the choices that follow, describe your response in the space provided.

a. Confront the official and stand up for Kandace. Tell the official that he blew the call and deserved Kandace's comments.

b. Confront the official and plead for mercy. Tell him that Kandace just got caught up in the moment and didn't mean any harm.

c. Pull Kandace aside while the opposing team shoots the technical fouls and read her the riot act. However, leave her in the game because you need her points to have any chance of winning the game.

d. Escort Kandace to the end of the bench and tell her that's her seat for the rest of the game. After the game, remind your team of the importance of respecting authority. Deal with Kandace in a private meeting with her parents and your athletic director.

e. (add your response)

Activity 2.2   Athletes First, Winning Second—SAMPLE SOLUTION

Scenario 1: Playing Time

1. What would you do? How would you respond to John? If you'd respond differently from the choices that follow, describe your response in the space provided.

   a. Tell John that you understand why quitting might be an understandable initial response, but that you don't believe he's a quitter. Ask him to think it over for a day or two. If at that point he still feels that he would not be happy as the backup quarterback, thank him for all he has done for your program and wish him well.

   Given his demonstrated dedication to the program in previous years, you owe John more than this passive "be on your way if you wish" response. His pride has taken a hit, so rather than simply letting him think about this matter on his own, ask John to meet with you daily to discuss the benefits of staying on the team. Also, enlist several of John's peers to encourage him to remain with the program. If you allow John to quit with no intervention, it will serve to reinforce his perception that he's of little value to the team and may as well walk away from it.

   b. Tell John that football is a team game and that this is varsity football and the best players play. He needs to accept his role as the backup quarterback and should keep in mind how frequently second stringers—due to starters' injuries or subpar performance—get a chance to impact a game and season.

   Rubbing John's nose in your decision to demote him serves no purpose and will likely deter any notion he might have had about remaining on the team. If you sincerely believe he can be a valuable backup and mentor to the new starting quarterback, provide several examples of similar NFL quarterback situations in the past. Note how the supplanted starter benefitted his team by embracing his new role.

   c. Tell John that although he won't start at quarterback, he can play a critical role on the team. Ask him to consider trying another position that suits his abilities and fills the team's needs. Note that although he won't be taking snaps from center he's still considered to be a leader by his peers, and that by embracing another role on the team he will strengthen that perception and the quality of the team.

   This solution will work if you have demonstrated to John through the course of his career that you have the best interests of both individual players and the team at heart in all the decisions you make. He will appreciate that you are looking out for him and want him to remain a vital member of the squad. And if he chooses this path, he will soon gain reinforcement from the amount of respect shown to him by his teammates and members of the community.

d. Explain to John that his leadership role on the team doesn't depend on his status as a starter. He is critical to the team's success. Tell John that how he responds to this situation will speak volumes about his character and how he will learn to face difficult situations in the future. Ask John to accept the backup role and to become a mentor coach for the transfer quarterback and his teammates.

Sport offers the opportunity to grow as a person. The life lessons that can be learned in situations such as this will pay dividends to John far into his future. If John responds positively in this situation, he will be better prepared to handle similar challenges down the road.

e. (add your response)

Scenario 2: Problem Parent

1. What would you do? If you'd respond differently from the choices that follow, describe your response in the space provided.

a. Confront Fred in private and tell him that his comments are not welcome. Tell him that if he keeps it up, you're going to kick his daughter off of the team.

Talking to Fred about the problem in private is a good and apparently necessary first step. But matching Fred's poor manner of communication with similarly disrespectful and threatening responses of your own is hardly a solution to the matter. Instead, in the meeting convey to Fred that you have his daughter's and her team's best interests at heart. Ask Fred to explain specifically what action you have taken that would cause him to believe otherwise. If it turns out that Fred can be satisfied only if his daughter receives special attention, ask him to consider what such preferential treatment would mean for her future and what happens when he (Fred) can't force his will on others. Never use threats; they only show weakness and never result in a positive outcome for anyone involved.

b. Wait for the right moment during a game when Fred is mouthing off and call a time-out. Ask your athletic director to remove Fred from the school property, and ban him from the rest of your games. Make sure everyone in the stands hears your request!

Two wrongs don't make a right! If you confront Fred in public, what message are you sending to your players? Is this how you would want them to respond? What message are you sending to your athletic director? Are you modeling the behavior he expects of you as a coach? Moreover, think of the humiliation this will bring to Fred's daughter. That experience would leave a scar, and Fred would likely insist that she leave the team. In short, that's a losing response for all.

c. Ask Fred if he's interested in becoming an assistant coach.

There is some merit to this solution, especially if he is knowledgeable about the game, but it could make matters worse! If you can't communicate effectively with Fred as a parent, will you be able to control him as your assistant coach? Think carefully about what role you want him to play and what type of influence he will be before you put a whistle around his neck.

d. Call Fred at home and ask him for a private meeting in your office. Ask your athletic director to attend the meeting. When Fred arrives, thank him for coming and ask him about his playing career. Explain that you are concerned about Sue. She is losing her confidence and seems to be depressed most of the time. Tell Fred that you believe his comments and actions are having a negative effect on Sue and that you want to work things out to solve the problem. Let Fred know that your first concern is the well-being of his daughter.

Talking to Fred about the problem is a good step, and having your athletic director attend lets Fred know the severity of the problem. Start the meeting by acknowledging Fred's accomplishments as a player and then let him know that his daughter is your first priority as a coach. Your job is to convince Fred that your philosophy of athletes first and winning second will provide Sue with an avenue to be the best she can be!

e. (add your response)

Scenario 3: Hot Head

1. What would you do? If you'd respond differently from the choices that follow, describe your response in the space provided.

   a. Confront the official and stand up for Kandace. Tell the official that he blew the call and deserved Kandace's comments.

   Coaches should stand up for their players, but never when they are wrong. Nor is it appropriate to mouth off to an official. By failing to demonstrate proper respect, you are encouraging players to respond just as Kandace did, and that kind of behavior cannot be condoned.

   b. Confront the official and plead for mercy. Tell him that Kandace just got caught up in the moment and didn't mean any harm.

   This isn't a judgment call concerning the rules of the game; it's a matter of respecting authority. Pleading for mercy isn't going to change the official's mind and will only delay the message you need to send to Kandace. A simple apology on behalf of your player is appropriate, but even more important is to reinforce your preseason pronouncement that you will tolerate no negative behavior toward officials. Kandace needs to accept the consequences of her inappropriate actions.

   c. Pull Kandace aside while the opposing team shoots the technical fouls and read her the riot act. However, leave her in the game because you need her points to have any chance of winning the game.

   This response sends a mixed message to Kandace. You're upset about her actions, but not to the point of jeopardizing the outcome of the game. If you let her continue, you're telling her and the community that winning at any cost is your priority! Also, by demonstrating your own inappropriate manner of handling this matter with a player in the public eye, you have compromised whatever respect and authority you might have brought to the situation.

d. Escort Kandace to the end of the bench and tell her that's her seat for the rest of the game. After the game, remind your team of the importance of respecting authority. Deal with Kandace in a private meeting with her parents and your athletic director.

Though this may be an acceptable solution, the need to take such actions demonstrates some deficit in your preparation of players for competition. Assigning Kandace a seat on the bench might discourage her from acting similarly in subsequent games, but such lessons can get lost on young players. They will benefit more from observing proper, positive decorum on the bench and only respectful interactions with officials.

e. (add your response)

Activity 2.3 Coaching Successfully

Instructions

1. Use the Developmental Dozen table on page 21 to complete this activity.
2. Work individually.
3. Review the 12 coach-development goals in column 1 of the table and compare them with the related athlete-development goals in column 2.
4. In column 3, write a few words that describe your reaction to each coach-development goal. The words should describe what you honestly think about each goal, such as "agree," "disagree," "good," "bad," "easy to do," "hard to do," "need to do," "great," "I need to work on," "never thought of that."
5. Take three minutes to complete the activity.

C. Examining Coaching Styles

(Notes)

Activity 2.4 Part 1 Your Favorite Coach

Instructions

1. Work individually.
2. Think about your favorite coach. Think about how he or she coaches. What's his or her style? How does he or she behave and act toward the athletes?
3. Write three words that describe the characteristics of the coach's style.
4. Take two minutes and prepare to describe the coach's style to the class.

Developmental Dozen

Coach-development goals What should I do to improve my ability to coach successfully and help my athletes develop?	Athlete-development goals What athletes should achieve	My reaction
1. Define my coaching philosophy and style: Develop and refine my coaching philosophy and style.	**1. Have fun.**	
2. Develop character: Model, teach, and expect appropriate citizenship behaviors.	**2. Develop character.**	
3. Communicate effectively: Model, teach, and expect honest and effective communication.	**3. Communicate effectively.**	
4. Guide athletes to develop self-confidence: Model and teach self-confident attitudes and behaviors and create situations in which athletes experience success.	**4. Develop self-confidence.**	
5. Teach the sport effectively: Teach the rules, systems, and defined plays of the sport.	**5. Learn the sport.**	
6. Teach technical skills effectively: Teach correct and safe techniques.	**6. Perform technical skills well and safely.**	
7. Teach sport decision-making skills effectively: Model and teach perception, attention, and concentration skills.	**7. Learn sport decision-making skills.**	
8. Teach tactical skills effectively: Teach athletes how to process game situations to provide competitive advantage.	**8. Execute tactical skills well.**	
9. Challenge athletes in practice and competition: Develop season and practice plans to create optimally challenging, safe, and effective practices and competitions.	**9. Strive to be better in practice and competition.**	
10. Physically prepare athletes: Model, teach, and expect appropriate physical training, nutrition, and drug-free habits.	**10. Value physical preparation.**	
11. Manage relationships effectively: Model, teach, and expect positive interactions with coaches, athletes, parents, administrators, medical personnel, officials, and media.	**11. Manage relationships effectively.**	
12. Support scholastic achievement: Expect commitment to academics and teach the value of education.	**12. Achieve scholastic potential.**	

DVD 3 Styles of Successful Coaches

(Notes)

Activity 2.4 Part 2 Your Favorite Coach

Instructions

1. As a class, we'll compare the coaching styles of your favorite coaches with the coaching styles described in the DVD.

(Notes)

D. Unit Summary

(Notes)

Test Preparation

Complete these steps as you prepare to take the test:

1. Read the following chapters in *Successful Coaching*:
   - Chapter 1 Developing Your Coaching Philosophy
   - Chapter 2 Determining Your Coaching Objectives
   - Chapter 3 Selecting Your Coaching Style
   - Chapter 4 Coaching for Character
   - Chapter 5 Coaching Diverse Athletes
2. Complete the units related to principles of coaching in *Coaching Principles Online* component.

Coaching Successfully

1. Read the code of ethics that your instructor handed out or referred you to.
2. List other tips from the instructor here.
3. Review the coach-development goals addressed in this unit and included in the table on page 23.
4. Use the space provided to briefly explain
   - what you learned in this unit about the goals, and
   - what you feel you should do *to improve your ability to coach successfully and help your athletes develop* by achieving these goals.
5. After the course, revisit this page and add notes that help you develop your coaching knowledge and career.

Developmental Dozen

Coach-development goals What should I do to improve my ability to coach successfully and help my athletes develop?	Athlete-development goals What athletes should achieve
1. Define my coaching philosophy and style: Develop and refine my coaching philosophy and style.	**1. Have fun.**
2. Develop character: Model, teach, and expect appropriate citizenship behaviors.	**2. Develop character.**

Principles of Management

PURPOSE To help you manage your relationships with people involved in the sport program, to help you meet your risk-management responsibilities and legal duties, and to help you manage your time.

Learning Objectives

In this unit you will learn

- the importance of managing relationships with parents, other coaches, administrators, officials, and other people involved in the sport program;
- about your responsibility to manage the risks associated with the sport program and to comply with your 10 legal duties; and
- how to manage time in order to plan, organize, and manage the team.

UNIT OVERVIEW

Topic	Activities	Time (min)
A. Unit Introduction	Unit introduction Coaching Successfully notes	5
B. Relationship Management	Section introduction DVD 4 Managing Relationships Activity 3.1, Part 1 Relationships Matter Activity 3.1, Part 2 The Relationship List	25
C. Risk Management	Section introduction DVD 5 Managing Risk Activity 3.2 10 Legal Duties	15
D. Time Management	Section introduction Activity 3.3 Time Well Spent	15
E. Unit Summary	Unit summary Coaching Successfully tips Coaching Successfully notes	5
TOTAL MINUTES		**65**

A. Unit Introduction

In unit 3 we'll discuss the principles of management. We'll cover these principles in three sections: relationship management, risk management, and time management.

- Sections one and two start with a DVD.
  - The first DVD discusses the interpersonal skills you'll use to manage the relationships with the people around you and the sport program.
  - The second DVD discusses your responsibilities to manage the risks of the sport program—for example, responding to an athlete's injury—and to comply with 10 legal duties.
- When we've completed this unit, you should be able to
  - describe why effectively managing relationships with your athletic director, parents, other coaches, administrators, officials, and other people involved in the sport program leads to highly respected program leadership;
  - explain your responsibilities to manage the risks associated with the sport program and to comply with your 10 legal duties; and
  - define daily coach-related priorities and time required to complete them.
- **Remember to update your Coaching Successfully notes related to coach-development goal 11, Manage Relationships Effectively.**

B. Relationship Management

(Notes)

DVD 4 Managing Relationships

(Notes)

Activity 3.1 Part 1 Relationships Matter

Instructions

1. Use the scenario that follows these instructions.
2. Work in teams.

3. Select a spokesperson to take notes and present the team's answers to the class.

4. Read the scenario, and discuss and answer the questions posed. Document your answers in the table on page 28 that follows the questions.

5. You'll have about 10 minutes for this activity.

6. When you're done, you should have read the scenario and answered two questions about it.

Relationships Matter

Sam is a sophomore and is new to Montgomery High School, having just moved to the area from another state. He loves soccer and has played on a travel team for the past four years and is looking forward to playing on the varsity squad this fall. He learns that there is a preseason camp at a nearby facility where the boys will stay overnight for three nights. Sam is excited that he will actually meet some of his fellow students before school even starts. Sam wants to fit in and be liked by his teammates, so after the first day at camp, he calls his older brother and asks him to bring him a case of beer. After Sam gets the beer from his brother, one of the assistant coaches finds Sam walking with the case behind the dorm where they are staying.

The coach confronts Sam and informs him that this is a serious violation of school and team policy. He has Sam open and empty every beer can. He calls the head coach and arranges to have a meeting. On the spot the head coach tells Sam that he is "retarded" for bringing beer to the preseason camp and informs him that he is off the team and that he needs to call his parents and get picked up.

The next day the head coach gets a call from his athletic director asking what happened with Sam. The athletic director tells the coach that Sam's mother was so upset about the incident—that her son was called "retarded" and in general how it was handled—that she called the superintendent, who in turn called the athletic director. She cited the school policy that says a student who commits a first offense of this nature will be forced to miss one third of the season but can continue to practice with the team. The athletic director is not happy that he heard about this from the superintendent and demands to meet with the coach right away.

1. Who are the people affected by Sam's actions and the coach's decision?

2. What should the head coach have done differently?

People affected	Recommendations for the head coach

Activity 3.1   Part 1 Relationships Matter— *SAMPLE SOLUTION*

1. Who are the people affected by Sam's actions and the coach's decision?
2. What should the head coach have done differently?

People affected	Recommendations for the head coach
Sam (athlete)	We don't have details on whether the team had yet met to review policies, but if they hadn't, such a meeting would be important. When the incident occurred, the coach should not have called Sam "retarded."
Sam's parents	After consulting with the athletic director (see below), it would have been advisable for the coach to call the parents and let them know what happened, send Sam home, and schedule time to meet with the parents, Sam, the assistant coach, and the athletic director.
Athletic director	A call to the athletic director would have been a good first step to 1. let him know the incident occurred, 2. discuss the best way to approach the situation, 3. ensure support from the athletic director for the coach's actions, and 4. allow the athletic director to contact the superintendent and inform him of the incident.
Superintendent	If the coach contacted the athletic director and they agreed on the consequence and how they would communicate to the parents, it is likely that the mother would not have contacted the superintendent. But in the worst-case scenario, the superintendent would have been contacted by the athletic director before the mother's call, allowing the superintendent to be prepared for the call.
Assistant coaches	Keep them engaged in the process.
Team	We don't have details on whether the team had yet met to review policies, but if they hadn't, such a meeting would be important. At some point the coaching staff should address the entire team regarding what happened and the corresponding consequences.
School principal	Work with the athletic director to communicate this incident to the principal.

Activity 3.1   Part 2 The Relationship List

Instructions

1. Use the Relationship List worksheet that follows these instructions. This worksheet is designed to help you identify the key people with whom you will interact so that you can take steps to establish positive working relationships.

2. Work individually.

3. List up to seven people with whom you expect to interact regularly in your role as coach.

4. Rank each relationship in order of importance as it relates to helping you be a successful coach.

5. You'll have about four minutes for this activity.

6. When you're done, you should have a completed and ranked relationship list.

Relationship List

Person	Order of importance

 Risk Management

(Notes)

DVD 5   Managing Risk

(Notes)

Activity 3.2   10 Legal Duties

Instructions

1. Use the Coaches' 10 Legal Duties list and the What the Coach Said form that follow the instructions to complete this activity.
2. Work in teams.
3. Select someone to record the team's answers.
4. For each quotation in column 1 of the form, determine which duty it relates to from the list of legal duties. Write the duty number in the second column.
5. You'll have five minutes to complete this activity.
6. When you're done, you should have indicated which legal duty relates to each quotation.
7. Finally, take a minute to review the Legal Duties Inventory form on page 34. Each school will have its own policies, procedures, resources, and responsibilities related to how coaches should comply with the 10 legal duties. Use this form to guide a discussion with your athletic administrator or head coach to determine what you will be expected to do for each duty.

Coaches' 10 Legal Duties

1: Properly plan the activity.	6: Match your athletes appropriately.
2: Provide proper instruction.	7: Evaluate athletes for injury or incapacity.
3: Warn of inherent risks.	8: Supervise the activity closely.
4: Provide a safe physical environment.	9: Provide appropriate emergency assistance.
5: Provide adequate and proper equipment.	10: Protect against physical and psychological harm from others.

What the Coach Said

Quotation	Legal duty
A. "Even though several athletes on my track team participated last year, they still need to have a preseason physical this year."	
B. "My athletic director approved the use of volunteer assistants, which allows me to give more individualized attention to all our athletes."	
C. "When we're doing drills, I don't have a problem matching a sophomore with a senior, as long as they're of similar skill and size."	
D. "One of my athletes suffered a concussion during practice. We employed our standard procedure and sent him to the emergency room for observation. I filled out our medical incident report forms and worked with our medical team to monitor the athlete for return to play, which took another two weeks."	
E. "Last week we were scheduled to play at a city park field because our urban school doesn't have a softball field. It rained all day, but the rain stopped by the time the game was scheduled. However, the field was a mess. I've never seen so much mud, and leaves and twigs were strewn all over. I asked the other coach if she and her team would help me and my team clean up the mess and together we got the field cleaned up and ready for play."	
F. "While equipment manufacturers have a responsibility to provide safe equipment, we do regular checks of all the equipment our players use in order to ensure that we minimize any risk of injury."	
G. "Believe me, we are fortunate to have a relationship with the golf course where our team plays. I make sure that the team understands their responsibility to maintain a safe distance from one another while taking full swings on the range. There can't be any foolin' around and I always stay at the course until the last player is picked up from practice. One player's bad or unsafe behavior could jeopardize our team's ability to practice and play there."	
H. "It's critical to include a description of risks for injury in the player handbook that is given out to each athlete to start the season. Our staff also covers this in our parent orientation meeting."	
I. "Sometimes my athletes and I become bored with the same old routines, so I let them work on advanced dives if the athletes are ready to start learning them."	
J. "My first year of coaching, the team captains came into my office and asked if they could do a little 'harmless initiation stuff' with their new teammates, like 'extra laps and no showers after practice.' I told them no, that there are more positive ways to create a sense of team and that what often starts out as 'harmless' can turn bad. There is no room for what amounts to negative initiation activity in our program."	

Activity 3.2   10 Legal Duties—SAMPLE SOLUTION

What the Coach Said

Quotation	Legal duty
A. "Even though several athletes on my track team participated last year, they still need to have a preseason physical this year."	7
B. "My athletic director approved the use of volunteer assistants, which allows me to give more individualized attention to all our athletes."	2
C. "When we're doing drills, I don't have a problem matching a sophomore with a senior, as long as they're of similar skill and size."	6
D. "One of my athletes suffered a concussion during practice. We employed our standard procedure and sent him to the emergency room for observation. I filled out our medical incident report forms and worked with our medical team to monitor the athlete for return to play, which took another two weeks."	9
E. "Last week we were scheduled to play at a city park field because our urban school doesn't have a softball field. It rained all day, but the rain stopped by the time the game was scheduled. However, the field was a mess. I've never seen so much mud, and leaves and twigs were strewn all over. I asked the other coach if she and her team would help me and my team clean up the mess and together we got the field cleaned up and ready for play."	4
F. "While equipment manufacturers have a responsibility to provide safe equipment, we do regular checks of all the equipment our players use in order to ensure that we minimize any risk of injury."	5
G. "Believe me, we are fortunate to have a relationship with the golf course where our team plays. I make sure that the team understands their responsibility to maintain a safe distance from one another while taking full swings on the range. There can't be any foolin' around and I always stay at the course until the last player is picked up from practice. One player's bad or unsafe behavior could jeopardize our team's ability to practice and play there."	8
H. "It's critical to include a description of risks for injury in the player handbook that is given out to each athlete to start the season. Our staff also covers this in our parent orientation meeting."	3
I. "Sometimes my athletes and I become bored with the same old routines, so I let them work on advanced dives if the athletes are ready to start learning them."	1
J. "My first year of coaching, the team captains came into my office and asked if they could do a little 'harmless initiation stuff' with their new teammates, like 'extra laps and no showers after practice.' I told them no, that there are more positive ways to create a sense of team and that what often starts out as 'harmless' can turn bad. There is no room for what amounts to negative initiation activity in our program."	10

Legal Duties Inventory

10 legal duties	Policies, procedures, resources, and responsibilities
Duty 1: Properly plan the activity.	
Duty 2: Provide proper instruction.	
Duty 3: Warn of inherent risks.	
Duty 4: Provide a safe physical environment.	
Duty 5: Provide adequate and proper equipment.	
Duty 6: Match your athletes appropriately.	
Duty 7: Evaluate athletes for injury or incapacity.	
Duty 8: Supervise the activity closely.	
Duty 9: Provide appropriate emergency assistance.	
Duty 10: Protect against physical and psychological harm from others.	

D. Time Management

(Notes)

Activity 3.3   Time Well Spent

Instructions

1. Use the Time Well Spent steps that follow these instructions and the table on page 36 to complete this activity.
2. Work individually.
3. Complete the four steps, and document your responses to steps two through four in the table on page 36.
4. You'll have six minutes to complete this activity.
5. When you're done, you should have listed and prioritized your weekly activities and indicated how much time you'll spend on each activity.

Time Well Spent

1. Indicate how many hours per week you expect to have available for your role as coach.
2. List up to seven activities that are necessary as part of your weekly plan for a successful season.
3. Prioritize the activities.
4. Estimate the amount of time you expect to spend each week on each activity.

E. Unit Summary

(Notes)

Test Preparation

Complete these steps as you prepare to take the test:

1. Read the following chapters in *Successful Coaching:*
   - Chapter 18 Managing Your Team
   - Chapter 19 Managing Relationships
   - Chapter 20 Managing Risk
2. Complete the units related to principles of management in *Coaching Principles Online Workbook.*

Coaching Successfully

1. Review the Parent Orientation Program Agenda and the Postseason Parent Evaluation form in chapter 19 in your text, *Successful Coaching,* and consider how you can use

Weekly activities	Priority	Time
1.		
2.		
3.		
4.		
5.		
6.		
7.		

them to learn more about what the parents of your athletes value in their children's sport programs and in their children's coach.

2. Review all of the forms in chapter 20 in your text, *Successful Coaching,* and consider if you should discuss them when you talk with your athletic administrator or head coach about your 10 legal duties.

3. Talk to your athletic administrator or head coach about your 10 legal duties using the Legal Duties Inventory form from Activity 3.2, 10 Legal Duties, in unit 3.

4. List other tips from the instructor here.

5. Review the coach-development goal addressed in this unit and included in the table at the bottom of this page.

6. Use the space provided to briefly explain

   • what you learned in this unit about the goal, and

   • what you think you should do *to improve your ability to coach successfully and help your athletes develop* by achieving this goal.

7. After the course, revisit this page and add notes that help you develop your coaching knowledge and career.

Developmental Dozen

Coach-development goals What should I do to improve my ability to coach and help my athletes develop?	Athlete-development goals What athletes should achieve
11. Manage relationships effectively: Model, teach, and expect positive interactions with coaches, athletes, parents, administrators, medical personnel, officials, and media.	**11. Manage relationships effectively.**

Principles of Physical Training

PURPOSE To help you understand your role in managing the physical preparation of your athletes.

Learning Objectives

In this unit you will learn about

- your role in managing the physical preparation of your athletes.

UNIT OVERVIEW

Topic	Activities	Time (min)
A. Unit Introduction	Unit introduction Coaching Successfully notes	5
B. Ensuring Athletes' Physical Preparation	Section introduction Activity 4.1 Physical Preparation Quiz DVD 6 Physical Fitness Activity 4.2 Managing the Physical Preparation of Your Athletes	20
C. Unit Summary	Unit summary Coaching Successfully tips Coaching Successfully notes	5
TOTAL MINUTES		**30**

A. Unit Introduction

In unit 4 you'll learn about your role in managing the physical preparation of your athletes.

- This unit introduces you to the basics. When you read *Successful Coaching* after the class, you'll learn about the specifics and you'll learn how to use a variety of tools that will help you succeed.
- This unit has one primary section: Ensuring Athletes' Physical Preparation.
    - It begins with an activity that will test your understanding of some physical preparation concepts.
    - After the activity, we'll watch a DVD that provides an overview of the basics of physical fitness.
    - This unit concludes with an activity that should get you started on managing the physical preparation of your athletes.
- When we've completed this unit, you should be able to describe your role in managing the physical preparation of your athletes.
- **Remember to update your Coaching Successfully notes related to coach-development goal 10, Physically Prepare Athletes.**

B. Ensuring Athletes' Physical Preparation

(Notes)

Activity 4.1 Physical Preparation Quiz

Instructions

1. Use the Physical Preparation Quiz that follows these instructions.
2. Work individually.
3. Answer the quiz questions.
4. You'll have three minutes to complete this activity. Complete as much of the quiz as you can.
5. When you're done, you should have answered 10 questions.

Physical Preparation Quiz

1. The human body has how many muscles?
   a. 120
   b. 240
   c. 360
   d. 480
   e. 640

2. Which is NOT a benefit of physical training?
   a. better performance
   b. less susceptibility to injury
   c. more muscle soreness
   d. improved concentration
   e. greater self-confidence

3. At rest, what percentage of the body's energy is used by muscles and what percentage is used by the brain?
   a. 20% by muscles and 20% by the brain
   b. 40% by muscles and 20% by the brain
   c. 30% by muscles and 60% by the brain
   d. 50% by muscles and 50% by the brain

4. When first starting to exercise or when exercising intensely, which energy system supplies the primary energy to the body?
   a. respiratory
   b. muscular
   c. aerobic
   d. anaerobic

5. In resistance training (e.g., lifting weights), muscle soreness occurs
   a. from lifting the resistance
   b. from lowering the resistance
   c. from lifting and lowering the resistance

6. Which type of stretching before vigorous exercise helps performance and prevents injuries?
   a. ballistic stretching
   b. dynamic stretching
   c. static stretching
   d. all of the above

7. Which is NOT a basic nutrient?
   a. carbohydrate
   b. fat
   c. protein
   d. sugar
   e. water

8. Which basic nutrient provides the most calories of energy per gram?

   a. carbohydrate

   b. fat

   c. protein

9. For 8th-, 10th-, and 12th-grade students in the United States, which activity increased from 1999 to 2009?

   a. tobacco use

   b. illegal drug use

   c. abuse of prescription drugs

10. Smokeless tobacco

   a. can lead to nicotine addiction

   b. creates no cancer risk

   c. provides a competitive edge

Activity 4.1 Physical Preparation Quiz— SAMPLE SOLUTION

Physical Preparation Quiz

1. The human body has how many muscles?

   a. 120

   b. 240

   c. 360

   d. 480

   e. 640

2. Which is NOT a benefit of physical training?

   a. better performance

   b. less susceptibility to injury

   c. more muscle soreness

   d. improved concentration

   e. greater self-confidence

3. At rest, what percentage of the body's energy is used by muscles and what percentage is used by the brain?

   a. 20% by muscles and 20% by the brain

   b. 40% by muscles and 20% by the brain

   c. 30% by muscles and 60% by the brain

   d. 50% by muscles and 50% by the brain

4. When first starting to exercise or when exercising intensely, which energy system supplies the primary energy to the body?

   a. respiratory

   b. muscular

   c. aerobic

   d. anaerobic

5. In resistance training (e.g., lifting weights), muscle soreness occurs
   a. from lifting the resistance
   b. from lowering the resistance
   c. from lifting and lowering the resistance

6. Which type of stretching before vigorous exercise helps performance and prevents injuries?
   a. ballistic stretching
   b. dynamic stretching
   c. static stretching
   d. all of the above

7. Which is NOT a basic nutrient?
   a. carbohydrate
   b. fat
   c. protein
   d. sugar
   e. water

8. Which basic nutrient provides the most calories of energy per gram?
   a. carbohydrate
   b. fat
   c. protein

9. For 8th-, 10th-, and 12th-grade students in the United States, which activity increased from 1999 to 2009?
   a. tobacco use
   b. illegal drug use
   c. abuse of prescription drugs

10. Smokeless tobacco
    a. can lead to nicotine addiction
    b. creates no cancer risk
    c. provides a competitive edge

DVD 6 Physical Fitness

(Notes)

Activity 4.2 Managing the Physical Preparation of Your Athletes

Instructions

1. Review the list of topics on the Athletes' Physical Preparation: Questions to Ask form on the next two pages.

2. Work individually.

3. Take two minutes for your review.

4. As you review the list, use the space provided to identify the questions that are most important and relevant for your situation and which you will benefit from asking your athletic administrator or head coach.

C. Unit Summary

(Notes)

Test Preparation

Complete these steps as you prepare to take the test:

1. Read the following chapters in *Successful Coaching*:
   - Chapter 13 Training Basics
   - Chapter 14 Training for Energy Fitness
   - Chapter 15 Training for Muscular Fitness
   - Chapter 16 Fueling Your Athletes
   - Chapter 17 Battling Drugs

2. Complete the units related to principles of physical training in *Coaching Principles Online* component.

Coaching Successfully

1. Using the Athletes' Physical Preparation: Questions to Ask form from Activity 4.2, Managing the Physical Preparation of Your Athletes, in unit 4, talk to your athletic administrator or head coach about your role in managing the physical preparation of your athletes.

2. List other tips from the instructor here.

3. Review the coach-development goal addressed in this unit and included in the table on page 46.

4. Use the space provided to briefly explain
   a. what you learned in this unit about the goal, and
   b. what you feel you should do *to improve your ability to coach successfully and help your athletes develop* by achieving this goal.

5. After the course, revisit this page and add notes that help you develop your coaching knowledge and career.

Athletes' Physical Preparation: Questions to Ask

Successful Coaching chapter topics	Questions
Chapter 13 Training Basics	
How the body works	
Fitness for sport and physical training	
Coach's role in physical training	
• Know sport physiology and training methods	
• Determine the physical demands of your sport	
• Assess the fitness of your athletes	
• Design a physical training program	
• Educate your athletes about the training program	
• Conduct the training program	
Training principles	
Chapter 14 Training for Energy Fitness	
Energy and energy fitness	
Physiology of energy systems	
Energy demands of your sport	
Measuring energy fitness	
Designing an energy fitness training program	
• Training pyramid	
• Seasonal training plan for aerobic fitness	
• Types of exercise	
Chapter 15 Training for Muscular Fitness	
Muscular fitness defined	
How muscles work	
Flexibility training	
Resistance training	
Muscular demands of your sport	
Testing muscular fitness	
Designing a muscular fitness program	
• Flexibility training	
• Resistance training	
• Muscular endurance training	

> continued

Successful Coaching chapter topics	Questions
Chapter 15 Training for Muscular Fitness (continued)	
• Speed training	
• Power training	
Chapter 16 Fueling Your Athletes	
Coach's role	
Six basic nutrients	
The athlete's diet	
More about carbohydrate, protein, and fat	
Nutritional supplements	
Hydration	
How much to eat	
When and what to eat	
Eating disorders	
Chapter 17 Battling Drugs	
Drugs 101	
Your role in prevention	
• Take an antidrug stance	
• Be a role model	
• Establish and enforce rules	
• Educate your athletes	
• Team culture	
When athletes have a drug problem	

Developmental Dozen

Coach-development goals What should I do to improve my ability to coach successfully and help my athletes develop?	**Athlete-development goals** What athletes should achieve
10. Physically prepare athletes: Model, teach, and expect appropriate physical training, nutrition, and drug-free habits.	**10. Value physical preparation.**

Principles of Behavior

PURPOSE To help you understand the influence you can have on athletes by using effective communication, motivation, and discipline, and to help you coach athletes of all types in an environment of respect.

Learning Objectives

In this unit you will learn

- how to communicate positively with athletes,
- how to use motivation and discipline to guide athletes' behavior and to create an environment in which athletes can have fun and feel worthy, and
- how to manage relationships with athletes in an environment based on respect for the program and its athletes.

UNIT OVERVIEW

Topic	Activities	Time (min)
A. Unit Introduction	Unit introduction Coaching Successfully notes	5
B. Engaging and Encouraging Athletes	Section introduction DVD 7 Communication Activity 5.1 Effective Communication DVD 8 Positive Energy Activity 5.2 Positive Energy DVD 9 Positive Discipline Activity 5.3 Disciplining Athletes Activity 5.4 School Rules	60
C. Coaching Athletes of All Types	Section introduction DVD 10 Respect Your Program Activity 5.5 Athlete Relations Activity 5.6 A Little Respect	25
D. Unit Summary	Unit summary Coaching Successfully tips Coaching Successfully notes	5
TOTAL MINUTES		**95**

A. Unit Introduction

In unit 5 we'll discuss the principles of behavior. We'll cover these principles in the following two sections:

- Engaging and Encouraging Athletes starts with a DVD and an activity about effective communication and how to improve the ineffective communication of three coaches.
  - Then, in a DVD and a related activity, we'll discuss what motivates athletes most: having fun and feeling worthy. You'll learn why it's important to help athletes achieve what psychologists call optimal activation, or flow, and what we call positive energy.
  - In another DVD and a related activity, we'll cover disciplining athletes using positive, preventive, and corrective discipline. Then you'll consider how to discipline two groups of athletes, one you catch drinking and one you catch bullying another athlete.
  - Finally, we'll discuss why you should read and understand school rules specifically related to disciplining and rewarding athletes and generally related to your treatment of athletes.
- Coaching Athletes of All Types starts with a DVD about respecting your program.
  - Then in two activities, we'll discuss what you can do to manage your relations with athletes and to create an environment of respect.
- When we've completed this unit, you should be able to
  - identify the keys for communicating positively with athletes,
  - explain how to use motivation and discipline to guide athletes' behavior and to create an environment in which athletes can have fun and feel worthy, and
  - describe how to manage relationships with athletes in an environment based on respect for the program and its athletes.
- **Remember to update your Coaching Successfully notes related to coach-development goals 3, Communicate Effectively; 4, Guide Athletes to Develop Self-Confidence; and 12, Support Scholastic Achievement.**

B. Engaging and Encouraging Athletes

(Notes)

DVD 7 Communication

(Notes)

Activity 5.1 Effective Communication

Instructions

1. Use the Help the Coach form that follows these instructions to complete this activity.
2. Work in teams.
3. Select a spokesperson to take notes and present the team's answers to the class.
4. Determine which list of communication tips would help each coach in the DVD become a better communicator. Write the coach's name in the left column of the table.
5. You'll have five minutes to complete this activity.
6. When you're done, you should have filled in the three coach names in the table.

Help the Coach

Coach	Communication tips
_____	List 1 • Recognize that much of what you communicate is in the form of nonverbal messages. • Send and receive effective messages. Use and read body position, body motion, voice characteristics, and touching behaviors. • What you do influences athletes more than what you say. • Tell athletes how you plan to measure success and then provide feedback consistent with expectations. Provide positive feedback that reinforces achieving success on a skill or task that was a point of emphasis for improvement.

> continued

Coach	Communication tips
_____	**List 2** • Use language that your athletes will understand. Keep your vocabulary simple and straightforward. • Think through your demonstrations before you present them. Break skills down into a step-by-step process and then present them in an organized sequence. • Keep cues short and simple, such as "Stay on your man" or "Arms in the air." • Strive hard to be consistent in your verbal messages. Ensure that your nonverbal actions are consistent with your verbal messages. • Develop a sense of trust with your athletes by being consistent and positive. Through trust you become a coach of character. • When you promise to do something, be sure to follow through. • Show the person speaking to you that you're interested in listening and trying to understand. • Once someone has spoken to you, check that you understand what was said. Paraphrase not only the content of the message but also the emotion behind it. • By your attentiveness, show that you care and that you respect what the person speaking to you has to say.
_____	**List 3** • Provide positive feedback for actions related to sportsmanship goals that help athletes develop character. • Provide honest, direct, and constructive messages. • Tell athletes directly when you catch them doing good or right, and then share with their teammates. • Engage in conversations focused on what can be done, not on what cannot be done. • Where appropriate, collaborate with athletes on defining solutions to problems. • Provide specific information when communicating feedback to help athletes correct mistakes. Try to always use positive language, even in the most stressful and frustrating situations. Ask athletes to explain their actions before you judge their behavior.

Activity 5.1   Effective Communication—
SAMPLE SOLUTION

Help the Coach

Coach	Communication tips
Coach Clarmoore	**List 1** • Recognize that much of what you communicate is in the form of nonverbal messages. • Send and receive effective messages. Use and read body position, body motion, voice characteristics, and touching behaviors. • What you do influences athletes more than what you say. • Tell athletes how you plan to measure success and then provide feedback consistent with expectations. Provide positive feedback that reinforces achieving success on a skill or task that was a point of emphasis for improvement.
Coach Wrotten	**List 2** • Use language that your athletes will understand. Keep your vocabulary simple and straightforward. • Think through your demonstrations before you present them. Break skills down into a step-by-step process and then present them in an organized sequence. • Keep cues short and simple, such as "Stay on your man" or "Arms in the air." • Strive hard to be consistent in your verbal messages. Ensure that your nonverbal actions are consistent with your verbal messages. • Develop a sense of trust with your athletes by being consistent and positive. Through trust you become a coach of character. • When you promise to do something, be sure to follow through. • Show the person speaking to you that you're interested in listening and trying to understand. • Once someone has spoken to you, check that you understand what was said. Paraphrase not only the content of the message but also the emotion behind it. • By your attentiveness, show that you care about and respect what the person speaking to you has to say.
Coach Alito	**List 3** • Provide positive feedback for actions related to sportsmanship goals that help athletes develop character. • Provide honest, direct, and constructive messages. • Tell athletes directly when you catch them doing good or right, and then share with their teammates. • Engage in conversations focused on what can be done, not on what cannot be done. • Where appropriate, collaborate with athletes on defining solutions to problems. • Provide specific information when communicating feedback to help athletes correct mistakes. Try to always use positive language, even in the most stressful and frustrating situations. Ask athletes to explain their actions before you judge their behavior.

DVD 8   Positive Energy

(Notes)

Activity 5.2   Positive Energy

Instructions

1. Use the Coach Behaviors form that follows these instructions to complete this activity.
2. Work individually.
3. List three or four words or phrases that describe how coach 1 and coach 2 treated their athletes.
4. You'll have two minutes to complete this activity.
5. When you're done, you should have a list of words describing each coach's behavior.

Coach Behaviors

Coach Steele	Coach Thurston

Instructions

1. Use the Coach Evaluation table that follows these instructions to complete this activity.
2. Work individually.
3. Evaluate whether you think coaches 1 and 2 will have positive or negative effects on the attitudes and performance of their athletes. Add + for positive and – for negative in the blank cells in the table.
4. You'll have one minute to complete this activity.
5. When you're done, you should have evaluated each coach.

Coach Evaluation

Athletes' attitudes and performance	Coach Steele	Coach Thurston
Fun		
Feeling worthy		
Activation		
Performance		

Activity 5.2 Positive Energy—SAMPLE SOLUTION

Coach Evaluation

Athletes' attitudes and performance	Coach Steele	Coach Thurston
Fun	−	+
Feeling worthy	−	+
Activation	−	+
Performance	−	+

Tips for Making Sports Challenging and Exciting

You can help your athletes meet their need for fun by making the sport experience challenging and exciting, not boring or threatening. When athletes are bored, they don't have enough activation. When they are threatened to the point of anxiety, they are experiencing too much activation. As a coach, you can work to ensure that your athletes are neither bored nor fearful, because where you want them to be is between these two extremes—experiencing optimal activation or flow. It's a tall order, but it can be done. Here are some ideas for how to accomplish this.

A. What can coaches do to keep athletes from getting bored in practices and competitions?

- Keep practices stimulating by using a wide variety of drills and activities to work on skills.
- Keep everyone active rather than standing around for long periods while waiting for their turns.
- Create a team environment that gives athletes the opportunity to interact with their teammates.
- Try not to overstructure practices and contests—this greatly reduces opportunities for players to be spontaneous.
- Try to create a practice environment that is not so competitive that players feel they are playing against each other rather than with each other.

B. What can coaches do to limit athletes' anxiety or fear of failure?

- Fit the difficulty of the skills to be learned or performed to the ability of the athletes.
- Help athletes set goals related to personal performance rather than to winning (coach to learn instead of coach to perform).

- Avoid putting the responsibility for winning a game on one athlete's shoulders.
- Use positive encouragement rather than negative or critical comments.
- Give feedback that is high in information rather than high in judgment (coach to learn instead of coach to perform).

C. What else can coaches do to help athletes experience optimal arousal and, thus, flow?

- Avoid constant instruction during practices and games.
- Refrain from continuous evaluation of your athletes, especially during competitions. Young athletes will not experience flow when they know they are being critiqued.

DVD 9   Positive Discipline

(Notes)

Activity 5.3   Disciplining Athletes

Instructions

1. You'll use the Smoking and Drinking scenario or the Hazing and Bullying scenario that follows these instructions.
2. Work in teams.
3. Select a spokesperson to take notes and present the team's answer to the class.
4. Read the scenario, and discuss and answer the question posed.
5. You'll have eight minutes for this activity.
6. When you're done, you should have responded to your assigned scenario and be prepared to share your answer with the class.

Disciplining Athletes

Scenario 1: Smoking and Drinking

Rules

Your school has a policy that forbids smoking, drinking, or use of illegal drugs on school property. Depending on the frequency and severity of the behavior, students can serve detentions, be suspended, or be expelled. The team rules for your girls' lacrosse team extends this policy to prohibit athletes from smoking, drinking, or using illegal drugs at any time. The rule clearly states that consequences for drinking and drug use can be assigned simply for being in the presence of such behavior. The first offense is a three-game suspension. Depending on the frequency and severity of the behavior, athletes can be removed from the team.

Situation

The girls' lacrosse team just won its fifth conference game in a row and has two regular-season games left before the conference tournament. If they win the remaining two games, they'll win the conference regular-season title and be the number-one seed for the tournament. After the game, six seniors—all starters—shower, get dressed in their prom gowns, and board a rented bus with their dates, headed for the prom. When they arrive, the prom chaperones—teachers and school administrators—board the bus to greet the girls and their dates. On the bus, the chaperones find a cooler with beer and wine, empty beer cans, soda cans, an open bottle of vodka, and an open bottle of whisky. Shortly after that, one of the chaperones calls you with the bad news.

1. What actions would you take in response to what the six starters did?

Scenario 2: Hazing and Bullying

Rules

Your school forbids hazing or bullying on school property, and the football team took it one step further by establishing a rule that hazing and bullying are not allowed anywhere at any time. In recent years the school took a progressive stance to include cyberbullying in the policies. Depending on the frequency and severity of the behavior, students can serve detentions, be suspended, or be expelled. The team rules for your boys' football team prohibit hazing or bullying of any kind toward any person. The rules also prohibit athletes from watching the hazing or bullying of anyone on or off school grounds. Depending on the frequency and severity of the behavior, athletes can be suspended or removed from the team.

Situation

As the head coach for the football team, you receive a call from the mother of Jerry, a freshman who is a shot putter on the high school's track team. The student has complained to his mother that members of the football team have been making fun of him for being a nerd and being fat. At lunch they take his lunch, throw it on the ground, step on it, hand it back to him, and tell him that he is so fat that he doesn't need the food. She goes on to say that before practice after school, about five players frequently corner Jerry in the hallway and taunt him, sometimes even slapping him in the face. She indicates that someone videotaped the players harassing her son and posted it to one of the player's Facebook page with the message "fat nerd of the day." Finally, she tells you that her son has been getting extremely hurtful e-mails and text messages from some of these players. She's asking for your help in addressing the matter.

1. What actions would you take in response to Jerry's allegations?

Activity 5.3 Disciplining Athletes—SAMPLE SOLUTION

Scenario 1: Smoking and Drinking

1. What actions would you take in response to what the six starters did?

   Given what you know, what you do should be based on the following principles:

   As the head coach, you should inform the athletic director when athletes break serious rules.

   Knowing that the chaperones included teachers and administrators, you and the athletic director should consult with these chaperones to gather the facts. You should also coordinate with the chaperones to inform the principal or other school administrators of this violation. The athletes weren't drinking or smoking on school property, but they were breaking the law and the team rule.

   As the head coach, work with the athletic director and other school administrators to define the approach and final consequences. One recommended approach is to gather the girls as quickly as possible and conduct individual interviews to gather facts from which to make informed and appropriate decisions. Whenever possible, you first should confront the athletes with the facts as you know them and try to determine what actually happened.

   Work with the athletic director to determine when and how you communicate with the parents of these athletes. Assume that the chaperones and school administrators have already notified the parents of this transgression, so your communication will relate specifically to the consequences resulting from the rules violation. If rules were broken, you should enforce them by applying the appropriate consequences—in this case, a three-game suspension for each player involved, which would mean missing the last two regular-season games and the first tournament playoff game.

Scenario 2: Hazing and Bullying

1. What actions would you take in response to Jerry's allegations?

   Assuming the mother's account is accurate, what you do should be based on the following principles:

   As the head coach, you should inform the athletic director that this alleged incident has been brought to your attention.

   As the head coach, work with the athletic director and other school administrators to define the approach and final consequences. One recommended approach is to gather the accused boys as quickly as possible and conduct individual interviews to gather facts from which to make informed and appropriate decisions. Whenever possible, you first should confront the athletes with the facts as you know them and try to determine what actually happened.

You and your athletic director should inform the principal or other school administrators when students break serious rules like this. In this case, it should be reported immediately because school and team rules were broken.

Work with the athletic director to determine when and how you communicate with the parents of these athletes. Your communication will relate specifically to the action and consequences resulting from the rules violation. If rules were broken, you should enforce them by applying appropriate consequences that are fair and consistent with the school and team policies. You need to be objective and assign consequences to the athletes consistently without any bias based on their importance to the team.

Activity 5.4   School Rules

(Notes)

C. Coaching Athletes of All Types

(Notes)

DVD 10   Respect Your Program

(Notes)

Activity 5.5   Athlete Relations

Instructions

1. With the quotations that the instructor read to you as background, list the dos and don'ts for managing your relationships with athletes of the opposite sex. For example, what's considered appropriate touching? Should or how should you conduct private meetings?

(Notes)

Coaching Recommendations

Follow these recommendations to avoid any implication or formal charges of sexual harassment, sexual relations, and homophobia on your program.

1. Not only must you not sexually harass your athletes or assistants, but you must also guard against any action that has the slightest appearance of harassment.

2. In addition to not engaging in sexual harassment, you have a duty as a coach not to let your athletes or assistants engage in this action. Watch for this especially with mixed-sex teams. In the past, sexual harassment has been dismissed as harmless teasing, but ignoring it sends a message that sexually abusing an athlete is acceptable behavior or at least not a serious matter.

3. Review the list in chapter five in *Successful Coaching* of what is considered harassment and review your behaviors as a coach to identify any actions that could possibly be interpreted as sexual harassment.

4. To avoid unintentional sexual harassment claims, discuss this issue at the preseason meeting with athletes and parents and ask them to notify you immediately if they experience or perceive any action on your part as harassment. And of course ask them to also notify you if they experience or perceive sexual harassment by another athlete or anyone associated with the team.

5. False accusation of sexual harassment has become an occupational hazard of employers and professionals, including coaches. Here are some things you can do to minimize the risk of being falsely accused:

   a. Try to always have others present when interacting with athletes. If that is not possible, leave the door open so it does not appear that you're trying to talk secretly.

   b. Be extra careful about any physical contact. Although psychologists call for more human contact (we all need more hugs), our litigious society makes touching risky. Sometimes you may need to touch athletes to guide their movements to learn a skill or treat an injury. Do so only with others present. Otherwise touch your athletes only in socially responsible ways. A pat on the fanny by a male coach to a male player is common, but it is not appropriate with a female player. A high-five or pat on the back is a wiser choice.

   c. If you accidentally touch an inappropriate body part during your coaching, don't just ignore it. Apologize and make it clear that the action was unintentional.

   d. If you are accused of sexual harassment, listen carefully to the complaint and don't try to make light of the accusation. Instead, respect the other person's viewpoint, identify the offending behavior, and stop it.

   e. Work with your sport administrator to develop a sexual harassment policy.

6. It is unethical, and perhaps illegal, for you to have sexual relationships with any athletes on your team. JUST DON'T DO IT!

7. Whenever possible, have another adult present when interacting with your athletes.

8. If the athlete is a consenting adult and you decide to have a sexual relationship with the athlete, either you or the athlete should resign from the team in the best interest of the other athletes.

9. Provide a safe and fair environment for athletes of all sexual orientations.

10. Apply the Athletes First, Winning Second approach by taking time to understand who your athletes are. If you have any existing prejudices, take steps to grow personally and professionally to eradicate those points of view, so you can treat all your athletes with the dignity and respect they deserve.

11. Establish and enforce policies that stop your athletes from engaging in antigay or homophobic behavior, explaining why it is harmful.

12. Consistently portray lesbians and gay people in neutral, matter-of-fact language.

13. Encourage your sport organization to adopt a nondiscrimination policy prohibiting bias, stereotyping, and harassment on the basis of sexual orientation.

Activity 5.6   A Little Respect

Instructions

1. You'll use the Different Cultural Backgrounds scenario or the Athlete With Cognitive Disabilities scenario that follows these instructions on page 60.

2. Work in teams.

3. Select a spokesperson to take notes and present the team's answer to the class.

4. Read the scenario, and discuss and answer the question posed.

5. You'll have five minutes for this activity.

6. When you're done, you should have responded to your assigned scenario and be prepared to share your answer with the class.

A Little Respect

Scenario 1: Different Cultural Backgrounds

Mike shows up for your first preseason workout and wants to try out for your basketball team. After watching him for just a few minutes, it's clear he's a talented athlete who could be a starter. He is a junior and has just moved to the United States from another country. At the end of the workout, as you work your way through the locker room as athletes shower and head out to catch their rides, you notice that no one is making an effort to speak with Mike. You have always talked to your team about the importance of respecting each other as teammates, but this group has never before played with someone from another country.

1. List five actions you can take as a coach to influence your team to get to know and respect Mike.

Scenario 2: Athlete With Cognitive Disabilities

Brian shows up at your preseason practices with great enthusiasm and ready to respond to your every command. He struggles to follow directions because he has learning disabilities associated with attention-deficit hyperactivity disorder. During practices, Brian shows some pretty good skills, but he often either doesn't appear to understand the strategy of the sport or fails to execute strategy correctly. You have concerns about his safety and his ability to have a meaningful experience. You also recognize that including him as a member of the team could be beneficial to him and to the rest of your team, but you're not sure if you can provide the type of teaching and coaching he will need throughout the season.

1. Describe steps that you could take that would help you decide whether or not to include Brian on your team.

2. Assume that you have decided to have Brian be part of the team. Describe steps to help accommodate Brian's needs and provide a meaningful experience for him and the rest of the team.

Activity 5.6 A Little Respect—SAMPLE SOLUTION

Scenario 1: Different Cultural Backgrounds

1. List five actions you can take as a coach to influence your team to get to know and respect Mike.

   a. Make a special point of talking with Mike about his basketball experience, his family, where's he's living, and the classes he's taking, and explain the team rules.

   b. Take the team out for a "welcome, Mike" snack. Have players introduce themselves and share a unique trait that not many people know.

   c. Follow the team policy of appointing an upperclass mentor to each new player. In this case, consider assigning one of the captains to take on this role, which includes helping Mike get acclimated to the team as well as the school.

   d. Ask the team captains to introduce themselves to Mike, ask if there's anything they can help him out with, and have them take a leadership role in inviting Mike to eat lunch with them and other teammates.

   e. Ask the team captains to encourage other athletes to have lunch with Mike, invite him out for a movie or other social function, and start to get to know him.

   f. Have team captains review team systems with Mike to accelerate his learning.

Scenario 2: Athlete With Cognitive Disabilities

1. Describe steps that you could take that would help you decide whether or not to include Brian on your team.

   a. Schedule a meeting with Brian's parents to discuss Brian's desire to be on the team and define the best way to provide a safe and healthy experience.

   b. Schedule a meeting with Brian's special education teacher to learn more about the type of environments in which Brian performs best. Ask if Brian has an individualized education program (IEP). If yes, ask the teacher to identify strategies and tactics that have been successful in connecting with Brian.

2. Assume that you have decided to have Brian be part of the team. Describe steps to help accommodate Brian's needs and provide a meaningful experience for him and the rest of the team.

   a. Meet with Brian individually and outline an individualized athlete development plan (IADP) that would work in much the same way as his IEP. Make sure he understands and agrees to his responsibilities and expectations.

   b. As much as possible, coach Brian just as you would anybody else, but make sure you have his attention when instructing, repeat the instruction several times, and invite Brian to summarize what you just said. Try teaching him some basic strategies and see if he catches on.

c. Understand that Brian may require more one-on-one teaching and coaching, so be committed to providing it.

d. In offering instruction or performance feedback, always make sure you have the athlete's attention before beginning.

e. Keep instructional or coaching points brief.

f. Repeat central instructional or coaching points.

g. Ask the athlete to repeat instructional points.

h. Meet with your team captains to discuss their role as team leaders to make sure that the team supports Brian and treats him as a respected member of the team.

i. Measure success by providing feedback during practice and with periodic one-on-one meetings to review his progress against the goals outlined in his IADP.

D. Unit Summary

(Notes)

Test Preparation

Complete these steps as you prepare to take the test:

1. Read the following chapters in *Successful Coaching*:
   - Chapter 6 Communicating With Your Athletes
   - Chapter 7 Motivating Your Athletes
   - Chapter 8 Managing Your Athletes' Behavior
2. Complete the units related to principles of behavior in *Coaching Principles Online* component.

Coaching Successfully

1. Evaluate your communication skills using the evaluation in the Evaluating Your Communication Skills section in chapter 6 in *Successful Coaching*. Consider how your communication strengths and weakness impact your ability to achieve your desired coaching style.

2. Read the Tips for Making Sports Challenging and Exciting from Activity 5.2, Positive Energy, in unit 5.

3. Review the websites that the instructor referred you to in unit 5 related to disciplining and rewarding athletes.

4. Read the school rules that the instructor handed out or referred you to in unit 5 for disciplining and rewarding athletes.

5. List other tips from the instructor here.

6. Review the coach-development goals addressed in this unit and included in the table at the bottom of this page.

7. Use the space provided to briefly explain

    a. what you learned in this unit about the goals, and

    b. what you feel you should do *to improve your ability to coach successfully and help your athletes develop* by achieving these goals.

8. After the course, revisit this page and add notes that help you develop your coaching knowledge and career.

Developmental Dozen

Coach-development goals What should I do to improve my ability to coach successfully and help my athletes develop?	**Athlete-development goals** What athletes should achieve
3. Communicate effectively: Model, teach, and expect honest and effective communication.	**3. Communicate effectively.**
4. Guide athletes to develop self-confidence: Model and teach self-confident attitudes and behaviors and create situations in which athletes experience success.	**4. Develop self-confidence.**
12. Support scholastic achievement: Expect commitment to academics and teach the value of education.	**12. Achieve scholastic potential.**

Principles of Teaching

PURPOSE To help you learn how to develop the technical and tactical skills of your athletes, to review the traditional and games approaches to coaching, to help you develop season plans, and to help you develop and evaluate practice plans.

Learning Objectives

In this unit you will learn

- how to teach technical and tactical sport skills effectively;
- how to evaluate and provide feedback for athletes' learning and performance;
- techniques for developing athletes' attention, concentration, and decision-making skills;
- the differences and similarities between the traditional and games approaches to coaching; and
- how to develop and evaluate a practice plan.

UNIT OVERVIEW

Topic	Activities	Time (min)
A. Unit Introduction	Unit introduction Coaching Successfully notes	5
B. Developing Athletes' Skill Sets	Section introduction DVD 11 Technical Skills Activity 6.1 Teaching Technical Skills DVD 12 Tactical Skills Activity 6.2 Attention and Concentration (With DVDs 13-16) DVD 17 Tactical Knowledge and Decision-Making Skills Activity 6.3 Teaching Tactical Skills	75
C. Creating Effective Practices	Section introduction DVD 18 The Games Approach Activity 6.4 Use What Works DVD 19 Annual, Season, and Practice Planning Activity 6.5 Practice Plan Evaluation	55
D. Unit Summary	Unit summary Coaching Successfully tips Coaching Successfully notes	5
TOTAL MINUTES		**140**

A. Unit Introduction

In unit 6 we'll discuss the principles of teaching. We'll cover these principles in the following two sections:

- Developing Athletes' Skill Sets starts with a DVD and a related activity about teaching the technical skills of your sport.
  - Then we'll watch a DVD about tactical skills. We'll also evaluate how well a coach did in improving his athletes' attention and concentration in four DVD clips of his practice session.
  - Next we'll watch a DVD and complete a related activity about teaching the tactical skills of your sport, including tactical knowledge and decision-making skills.
- Creating Effective Practices starts with a DVD and a related activity about using the games and traditional approaches to teach sport skills.
  - In the final DVD of the unit, we'll cover season and practice planning.
  - In the final activity of the unit, you'll evaluate a practice plan for your sport.

- When we've completed this unit, you should be able to
  - describe how to teach technical and tactical sport skills effectively;
  - evaluate and provide feedback for athletes' learning and performance;
  - identify techniques for developing athletes' attention, concentration, and decision-making skills;
  - discuss the differences and similarities between the traditional and games approaches to coaching; and
  - evaluate a practice plan.
- **Remember to update your Coaching Successfully notes related to coach-development goals 4, Guide Athletes to Develop Self-Confidence; 5, Teach the Sport Effectively; 6, Teach Technical Skills Effectively; 7, Teach Sport Decision-Making Skills Effectively; 8, Teach Tactical Skills Effectively; and 9, Challenge Athletes in Practice and Competition.**

B. Developing Athletes' Skill Sets

(Notes)

DVD 11 Technical Skills

(Notes)

Activity 6.1 Teaching Technical Skills

Instructions

1. You'll use the Technical Skill Teaching Plan form on page 69.
2. As indicated, work in teams of two to four coaches by sport. If you are the only coach for a particular sport, it is best for you to work individually on your sport.
3. Take notes and be prepared to present your plan to the class.
4. Quickly identify one technical skill from your sport to teach. This is step 1 on the form. If you have trouble identifying a technical skill, ask for help immediately.
5. Spend most of your time completing steps 2 through 7 on the Technical Skill Teaching Plan form. Your responses should describe your plan. It's OK to write only key words or short notes.
6. You'll have 10 minutes to complete this activity. Complete as much of your plan as you can.
7. When you're done, you should be ready to explain to the class how you would teach the technical skill you identified.

Sport Skills

Sport	Technical skill	Tactical skill
Baseball	Throwing from the outfield	Cutoff and relays
Basketball	Bounce pass	Give and go
Field hockey	Goal shooting	Lob or scoop shot
Football	Quarterback's three-step drop	Reading a flat defender
Golf	Full swing	Fade tee shot
Ice hockey	Forehand shot	Backdoor shot
Lacrosse	Shooting	Bounce shot
Skiing (alpine)	Carving a turn	See fast line through a delay
Skiing (cross country)	Balancing and gliding on one ski	Passing on a downhill
Snowboarding	Linking turns	Get angle for trick amplitude
Soccer	Passing	Flighted pass
Softball	Hitting	Hit and run
Swimming	Freestyle	Control, build, maintain, sprint
Tennis	Forehand	Drop shot
Track and field	Sprinter's start	Sprinting from the pack
Volleyball	High-outside set	Two-player serve–receive
Water polo	Two-hand save	Recognizing offenses
Weightlifting	Bench press	Maxing out
Wrestling	Single-leg attack	Reading a level change

Technical Skill Teaching Plan Evaluation Instructions

1. Refer to the Technical Skill Teaching Plan Evaluation form on pages 70-71.

2. As you listen to the other coaches' plans for teaching a technical skill, answer the questions on the form.

3. One coach will be asked to present the plan they designed by describing responses to steps 1 through 7 on the Technical Skill Teaching Plan form.

4. The instructor will ask other coaches if they have any questions or suggestions for the coach.

5. The instructor will continue reviewing plans, covering as many coaches as possible in the time available.

6. Carefully read chapter 10, Teaching Technical Skills, in *Successful Coaching* as you prepare for the test because this chapter provides a comprehensive overview.

Technical Skill Teaching Plan

1. Identify a technical skill from your sport to teach.
2. Determine whether you will teach the whole skill or break it into parts and teach the parts. If you decide to break it into parts, describe the parts.
3. Determine the approaches you will use to teach the skill. Describe what those approaches will look like, including the drills you will use and the games you might play.
4. Determine and list the teaching tips you will use during the mental stage of learning.
5. Identify the types of errors you expect to see during the mental stage, and explain the feedback approaches you will use for those errors.
6. Determine and list the teaching tips you will use during the practice stage of learning.
7. Identify the types of errors you expect to see during the practice stage, and explain the feedback approaches you will use for those errors.

Technical Skill Teaching Plan Evaluation

Criteria	Team 1	Team 2	Team 3
Teaching Approach			
What approach was used?			
Might a different approach have worked better?			
Mental Stage			
Was the number of teaching tips limited to avoid overload?			
Was a high number of errors expected?			
Practice Stage			
Were more teaching tips identified than were identified for the mental stage?			
Was feedback withheld when the learner would already sense his or her errors?			
Was positive reinforcement included for correct skill performance?			

Team 4	Team 5	Team 6	Team 7

DVD 12   Tactical Skills

(Notes)

Activity 6.2   Attention and Concentration (With DVDs 13-16)

Instructions

1. Use the Attention and Concentration worksheet that follows these instructions to complete the activity.

2. Work individually.

3. We'll watch four DVD segments of a basketball coach working with his team during a game.

4. After each segment, you'll answer the questions on the Attention and Concentration worksheet, and then we'll discuss what the coach did well and not so well.

5. When we're done, we'll have viewed four DVD segments and discussed the questions on the Attention and Concentration worksheet.

Attention and Concentration

Coach Pierce's team is taking a beating from their cross-town rival. His offense has been in trouble, mostly because the guards aren't making good decisions with the ball. When the guards receive passes, they aren't looking for cues while holding the triple-threat position. In the triple-threat position, the ball handler holds the ball and maintains a stance that allows him to shoot, dribble, or pass. This keeps the opponent guessing while the ball handler looks for cues as to what to do next.

Coach Pierce knows that it's not enough for him to simply explain moving from the triple-threat position. His players need to receive the ball and make good decisions quickly. He wants them to develop their ability to read the cues of the game.

First DVD Segment

1. How could Coach Pierce more effectively engage Cooper and retain his attention?
2. How does Coach Pierce's approach affect the concentration and attention of the other athletes?

Second DVD Segment

1. What's your initial reaction to Coach Pierce's approach?
2. Would you do anything differently?
3. How do his athletes seem to respond?

Third DVD Segment

1. How could Coach Pierce more effectively engage Cooper and retain his attention?
2. Could Coach Pierce use more positive language?
3. How does Coach Pierce's approach affect the concentration and attention of the other athletes?

Fourth DVD Segment

1. How could Coach Pierce more effectively engage Cooper and retain his attention?
2. How does Coach Pierce's approach affect the concentration and attention of the other athletes?
3. Do games provide teachable moments?

Activity 6.2 Attention and Concentration (With DVDs 13-16)—SAMPLE SOLUTION

First DVD Segment

1. How could Coach Pierce more effectively engage Cooper and retain his attention?

2. How does Coach Pierce's approach affect the concentration and attention of the other athletes?

   Coach Pierce was distracting Cooper, the guard, with advice while Cooper was playing.

   You should avoid distracting your athletes with comments while they're playing. You can still talk to them while they're on the court, but keep instructions simple, perhaps including reminders of earlier coaching points.

   Most coaches distract their players far too often and for the wrong reasons.

   In this case, Coach Pierce is trying to accomplish way too much in one shouted set of instructions while Cooper needs to be thinking about defense!

Second DVD Segment

1. What's your initial reaction to Coach Pierce's approach?

2. Would you do anything differently?

3. How do his athletes seem to respond?

   Coach Pierce used a teachable moment to give advice to a player.

   Instead of bombarding Cooper, the playing guard, with shouted, distracting advice, Coach Pierce used the teachable moment to teach the tactical decision point to the guard on the bench. When that guard substitutes in to the game, he will have had the opportunity to first think about the advice Coach Pierce gave him.

   Coach Pierce also might have suggested using a quick entry pass before the defense could recover rather than holding the triple-threat position. This demonstrates recognition of another opportunity.

Third DVD Segment

1. How could Coach Pierce more effectively engage Cooper and retain his attention?

2. Could Coach Pierce use more positive language?

3. How does Coach Pierce's approach affect the concentration and attention of the other athletes?

   Coach Pierce was right to wait for the time-out to give advice to his guard. Coach Pierce was wrong to give such public, negative feedback to his guard.

   The coach wasn't practicing positive coaching. Younger players tend to be especially vulnerable to distraction when their self-esteem is at risk. If you really want your players to learn the skills, you'll do more harm than good with this approach!

Fourth DVD Segment

1. How could Coach Pierce more effectively engage Cooper and retain his attention?

2. How does Coach Pierce's approach affect the concentration and attention of the other athletes?

3. Do games provide teachable moments?

   Coach Pierce was positive. He helped to put players' focus in the right place. Coach Pierce made a few great moves as he talked to his players, as follows:

   He helped them identify what to attend to (teammates, movement, guard spacing) and what to ignore (opposing forwards, crowd, score board).

   He delivered his comments to his guard in a "compliment sandwich."

   He encouraged his players to focus on the situation and their performance, not on the outcome (score board).

DVD 17 Tactical Knowledge and Decision-Making Skills

(Notes)

Activity 6.3 Teaching Tactical Skills

Instructions

1. You'll use the Tactical Skill Teaching Plan form that follows these instructions.

2. Work in teams. As we discussed with Activity 6.1, if you are the only coach for your sport, it is best for you to work individually on this activity.

3. For teams, select a spokesperson to take notes and present the team's plan to the class.

4. Quickly identify a tactical skill from your sport to teach. This is step 1 on the form. If you have trouble identifying a tactical skill, ask for help immediately.

5. Spend most of your time completing steps 2 through 6 on the Tactical Skill Teaching Plan form. Your responses should describe your plan. It's OK to write only key words or short notes.

6. You'll have 10 minutes to complete this activity. Complete as much of your plan as you can.

7. When you're done, you should be ready to explain to the class how you would teach the tactical skill you identified.

Tactical Skill Teaching Plan

1. Identify one tactical skill from your sport to teach your athletes. This tactical skill should be an important decision that your athletes need to make as they play the sport.

2. Identify the tactical knowledge your athletes need in order to decide when to use the tactical skill. Consider rules of the sport, the game plan, playing conditions, strengths and weaknesses of opponents, and the athletes' own strengths and weaknesses.

3. Identify a situation in which your athletes might use this tactical skill. For this situation, identify the cues your athletes should attend to in order to read the situation. Identify the cues that they should not attend to. Describe the situation and list both types of cues.

4. Identify the tactical options, guidelines, or rules your players should follow to use the tactical skill appropriately.

5. Design one practice game that would give your athletes the opportunity to practice decision-making skills by reading the situation and selecting the appropriate tactic.

6. Identify the types of errors you expect to see, and explain the feedback approaches you'll use for those errors.

C. Creating Effective Practices

(Notes)

DVD 18   The Games Approach

(Notes)

Activity 6.4   Use What Works

Instructions

1. You'll use the Use What Works form that follows these instructions. You'll also refer to your team's technical skill teaching plan in Activity 6.1 and your team's tactical skill teaching plan in Activity 6.3.
2. Work in teams.
3. Select a spokesperson to take notes and present the team's new plan to the class.
4. Quickly identify the skill your team will address. This is step 1 on the form.
5. If you selected the technical skill, complete step 2. If you selected the tactical skill, complete step 3. It's OK to write only key words or short notes.
6. You'll have 10 minutes to complete this activity. Complete as much as you can.
7. When you're done, you should be ready to explain to the class how you changed your approach to teaching the skill you identified.

Use What Works

1. Select **EITHER** the technical skill from your team's technical skill teaching plan from Activity 6.1 **OR** the tactical skill from your team's tactical skill teaching plan from Activity 6.3.

2. **IF** you chose the technical skill:

   - Use your teaching plan from Activity 6.1.

   - Summarize steps 1 and 2 of your plan.

   - Identify your teaching approach in step 3. Is it traditional, games, a combination of both, or something else?

   - Select a different approach for step 3 and describe it. It should be as effective as your first approach. IF it isn't as effective, or IF you think your first approach was better, explain why.

   - Review step 7. Revise the expected errors and feedback as necessary.

3. **IF** you chose the tactical skill:

   - Use your teaching plan from Activity 6.3.

   - Summarize steps 1 through 4 of your plan.

   - Identify your teaching approach in step 5. Is it traditional, games, a combination of both, or something else?

   - Select a different approach for step 5 and describe it. It should be as effective as your first approach. IF it isn't as effective, or IF you think your first approach was better, explain why.

   - Review step 6. Revise the expected errors and feedback as necessary.

DVD 19 Annual, Season, and Practice Planning

(Notes)

Activity 6.5 Practice Plan Evaluation

Instructions

1. You'll use the Practice Plan Evaluation form and one of the practice plans provided that follows these instructions. Evaluate a practice plan for your sport if possible.
2. Work in teams.
3. Select a spokesperson to take notes and present the team's evaluation to the class.
4. Review the practice plan.
5. Identify whether the practice plan includes each of the 11 components listed on the Practice Plan Evaluation form on page 80.
6. For components not included, describe how you would include the component in the plan.
7. You'll have eight minutes to complete this activity.
8. When you're done, you should have evaluated one practice plan and described how you will include the missing

Practice Plan Evaluation

Component	Component in plan?		If no, how could component be included?
	YES	NO	
Practice objectives are clearly stated.			
The format is easy to follow and contains pertinent information for each period.			
Practice time is used efficiently.			
A warm-up and stretching period is included.			
Ample breaks for fluid and rest are included.			
Periods for instruction of individual skill techniques are included.			
Athletes are given the opportunity to practice the techniques in game-like conditions.			
Periods for instruction of individual and team tactics are included.			
Athletes are given the opportunity to practice the tactics in game-like conditions.			
A cool-down period is included.			
A period for closing comments and announcements is included.			

Additional notes:

Practice Plan 1: Basketball

Date: December 12

Level: Varsity

Point in season: In-season

Practice start time: 2:45 p.m.

Length of practice: 115 minutes

Practice objectives: (1) Reinforce technical skills: dribbling, passing, shooting; (2) develop motion offense; and (3) work on transition defense.

Equipment: North Gym, six baskets, basketballs

PRACTICE ACTIVITIES

Time	Name of activity	Description	Key teaching points
2:45-2:50	Prepractice	Shoot 25 free throws and record number made.	Set percentage goal for each week.
2:50-3:00	Team stretch	Warm-up and stretching	Elevate heart rate. Dynamic stretching
3:00-3:02	Pitino Dribble drill	Jog, speed, cross, back	Keep eyes up. Push the ball ahead of you. Do not look at the ball.
3:02-3:08	Carolina Passing game	Passing game	Run at game speed. Pass and catch while saying the name of the passer or receiver on every pass.
3:08-3:14	Texas Conversion	Push tempo game	Make the easy pass. Get the ball to the basket.
3:14-3:20	3-on-3 Full-Court games	3 consecutive stops	Communicate on offense and defense. Offense: Pass and cut/screen; catch every pass ready to shoot (triple threat). Defense: Communicate screens; cut cutters; close out quickly with high hands; box out.
3:20-3:22	Free Throw drill	Shoot 4; 2 at a time; make 3 out of 4.	Elbow in front Wide thumb Ball on fingertips Find the W on the front of the rim. No stinkin' thinkin'!

> continued

Time	Name of activity	Description	Key teaching points
3:22-3:28	30-Second Shot drill	Shooter: Catch with inside pivot foot, show target; do not drop ball below point where you catch. Passer (rebounder): Pass to inside shoulder.	No talking; elbow to elbow. Right wing to right baseline; left wing to left baseline.
3:28-3:30	Drink break	Everyone drinks 4 to 8 oz sport drink or water.	
3:30-3:34	5-Man Weave	Pass and go behind 2 players. Middle players shoot at both.	Emphasize first opportunity attack; look for best attack in each rotation.
3:34-3:40	5-Man Weave Elimination	Rotate to your right 1 line. Last 2 to touch ball, back on defense.	
3:40-3:56	Jarvis Secondary Break	4-1-5 lob pass; run down mid. 4-1 make a move and penetrate. 4-1-4 for a shot, 1 screen for 2, etc.	Push the ball. 1 pass early to 5. 1 keep the ball. Make a move at the wing. Get to the basket. 1 push to wing, pass to 4 for a shot, and screen for 2.
3:56-4:04	Conditioning drill	Conditioning, building aerobic endurance	Pace yourself. Finish strong.
4:04-4:06	Drink break	Everyone drinks 4 to 8 oz sport drink or water.	
4:06-4:14	Basic 5-on-0	Man offense, 5-on-0, on the half court Practice entries: Wing entry High-post entry Dribble entry	Add screen and roll when go to corner. Work on timing and spacing.
4:14-4:25	Basic 5-on-5	Play 5-on-5 on the half court, working on the 3 entries. Defense has to get 3 stops to get on offense, and once they do, they run the secondary break 5-on-0 the other way. With a rebound or made basket, possession changes and players run the secondary break.	Proper spacing "Head hunt" on screens. Curl off of screens. Be patient when setting screens. Take proper angles when setting screens.

Time	Name of activity	Description	Key teaching points
4:25-4:30	Cool-down	Slow jogging, dribbling, easy play	
4:30-4:35	Cool-down and drink break	Main muscle group stretch Everyone drinks 4 to 8 oz sport drink or water.	Emphasize slow and complete stretch.
4:35-4:40	Coach's comments	End-of-practice comments from the coach	General comments on how the whole team practiced; recognize any outstanding efforts or performances; point out what the team needs to improve; announcements.

The basketball plan and its outcome (evaluation) were developed in collaboration with John Woods, athletic director, Champaign Central High School, Champaign, Illinois.

Practice Plan 2:   Football

Date: August 26

Level: Varsity; offensive practice

Point in season: Preseason; one week before first game

Practice start time: 3:45 p.m.

Length of practice: 135 minutes

Practice objectives: Solidify the basics for the first game of the season: opposing team's coverages and blitz package, pass protection, passing game, running game

Equipment: Stand-up and hand-held dummies, pull-overs, footballs

PRACTICE ACTIVITIES

Time	Name of activity	Description	Key teaching points
3:45-3:50	Prepractice	Special team walk through	Punt formation and assignments
3:50-4:00	Team stretch	Warm-up and stretching	Elevate heart rate. Dynamic stretching
4:00-4:05	Special teams practice: Punt team	Team 1. Spread punt 2. Tight punt	Interior line splits and footwork Personal protector responsibilities Wide out's alignment and release techniques Punter postpunt responsibilities
4:05-4:15	Run Blocking	WRs 1. Perimeter run plays 2. Inside run plays	Stance: Inside arm and leg back in sprinter's stance Start: Explode off the LOS and get in the DB's cushion. If the DB turns his hips and runs, run him off. If the DB squats, break down and attack his numbers. Keep a wide base with both your feet and hands.
4:15-4:18	Drink break	Everyone drinks 4 to 8 oz sport drink or water.	

Time	Name of activity	Description	Key teaching points
4:18-4:35	11-on-11 Running game	Team 1. 32 Dive vs. 50 Front 2. 32 Trap vs. 40 Front 3. 28 Sweep vs. 50 Front 4. 27 Sweep vs. 40 Front	O-line: Check alignment–stance–start before each play. Maintain blocks to the echo of the whistle. RBs: Check alignment–stance–start before each play. Lower your pad level, read your block, and run through arm tackles. QB: Check stance and footwork on each play. Look the ball into the RB's hands and carry out all run fakes. WRs: Check alignment–stance–start before each play. Stalk block the man over or greatest threat.
4:35-4:40	Drink break	Everyone drinks 8 oz sport drink or water.	
4:40-4:50	Blitz Package Walk Through	QB, HB, FB, O-line 1. 5-3 Mike Blitz 2. 5-3 Mike/Will Blitz 3. 4-4 Sam/Safety Blitz	O-line slide protection; center and FB read Mike. O-line slide protection; QB responsible for Will. O-line slide protection; tackles and HB responsible for Sam and Safety.
4:50-5:00	Blitz/Hot/Read Segment	Team 1. 5-3 Mike Blitz 2. 5-3 Mike/Will Blitz 3. 4-4 Sam/Safety Blitz	Slant route sight adjustment by HBs. Slant route sight adjustment by WRs and stop route by HBs. Stop route sight adjustment by FB and slant route sight adjustment by HBs. QB recognition, audible, and adjustment
5:00-5:05	Drink break	Everyone drinks 8 oz sport drink or water.	
5:05-5:15	5-Step Routes	QB, HBs, WRs 1. Michigan Right 2. 687-S-9 3. Dash Left 87	Option route read #2 strong. 6 route flat at 12 yards 7 route under 8 route

> continued

Time	Name of activity	Description	Key teaching points
5:05-5:15	Pass Protection	O-line 1. Slide Protection 2. Gangster Protection	Assignment Alignment Stance Footwork
5:15-5:25	11-on-11 Passing Game	Team 1. Michigan Right 2. 687-S-9 3. Dash Left 87	O-line: Slide protection rules and don't get beat to the inside. FB: Check pass-pro responsibility and check release. QB: Presnap read, then follow progression. Deliver the ball on time to the open receiver. HBs: Run designated route or check release if assigned. WRs: Run the routes at the proper depth, look the ball into your hands, and then look for positive yards.
5:25-5:30	Drink break	Everyone drinks 8 oz sport drink or water.	
5:30-5:50	Pressure Practice	Team 1. 32 Dive vs. 50 Front 2. 32 Trap vs. 40 Front 3. 28 Sweep vs. 50 Front 4. 27 Sweep vs. 40 Front 5. Michigan Right 6. 687-S-9 7. Dash Left 87	Ball on the +10-yard line, 1st and goal Perfect huddle Perfect alignment Perfect stances Perfect start Perfect play Score in the red zone.
5:50-6:00	Cool-down and drink break	Jogging and main muscle group stretch Everyone drinks 8 oz sport drink or water.	Emphasize slow and complete stretch.
6:00	Coach's comments	End-of-practice comments from the coach	General comments on how the whole team practiced; recognize any outstanding efforts or performances; point out what the team needs to improve; announcements.

The football practice plan was written by Coach Jerry Reeder, Eastern Illinois University.

Practice Plan 3:   Volleyball

Date: October 20

Level: Junior varsity

Point in season: In-season

Practice start time: 4:00 p.m.

Length of practice: 90 minutes

Practice objectives: (1) Practice core ball-control skills of passing and setting: flat forearm plat-forms that redirect the ball to the target (minimize swinging) and setting "hands position" at forehead early, with contact point on finger pads and thumbs closest to forehead; (2) enhance player communication: calling first ball ("me" or "mine"), where to attack (line or angle), and how many blockers are up against the hitter; (3) continue first opportunity attack emphasis, looking for one-on-one situations; and (4) develop physical recovery skills with short, intense physical bursts and timed recovery.

Equipment: Coach brings stopwatches, balls, net, and cones; players need knee pads and court shoes.

PRACTICE ACTIVITIES

Time	Name of activity	Description	Key teaching points
4:00-4:10	Warm-up	Shuffle Passing drill 10 to target and change direction	Emphasize posture and "quiet" passing platform.
4:10-4:20	Warm-up	Dynamic stretching	Emphasize full range of motion in stretches.
4:20-4:25	Drink break	Everyone drinks 4 to 8 oz sport drink or water.	
4:25-4:55	Ball control	Weave Passing drill in teams of 3; 15 to target (both sides)	Emphasize adjusting platform and movement to the ball.
4:55-5:00	Drink break	Everyone drinks 4 to 8 oz sport drink or water.	
5:00-5:03	Ball control	Line races (sprint, shuffle/back)	Physical training
5:03-5:18	6-on-6 Scrimmage	Attack or Tip/Roll	Emphasize first opportunity attack; look for best opportunity (1-on-1) to attack in each rotation. Can attack only when a 1-on-1 situation is created. If hitter has 2 or 3 blockers on her, she MUST tip or roll.

> continued

Time	Name of activity	Description	Key teaching points
5:18-5:23	Cool-down	Mat serving series	Emphasize serving routine and rhythm.
5:23-5:25	Cool-down and drink break	Main muscle group stretch Everyone drinks 4 to 8 oz sport drink or water.	Emphasize slow and complete stretch.
5:25-5:30	Coach's comments	End-of-practice comments from the coach	General comments on how the whole team practiced; recognize any outstanding efforts or performances; point out what the team needs to improve; announcements.

Practice Plan 4: Soccer

Date: August 25, hot and humid

Level: Varsity (high school)

Point in season: Fall preseason

Practice start time: 3:00 p.m.

Length of practice: 130 minutes

Practice objectives: (1) Continue to improve conditioning and speed endurance; (2) work on passing with a purpose: maintaining possession of the ball and improving players' tactical awareness off the ball; and (3) improve individual defending (tackling).

Equipment: Ideally one ball per player, goals or flags, cones and disc cones, scrimmage vests (at least two colors)

PRACTICE ACTIVITIES

Time	Name of activity	Description	Key teaching points
3:00-3:05	Warm-up	Easy jogging	
3:05-3:15	Warm-up	Dynamic stretching	Emphasize full range of motion.
3:15-3:20	Drink break	Everyone drinks 4 to 8 oz sport drink or water.	
3:20-3:30	Slalom drill	Stagger cones far apart for 180-degree turns; have players go as fast as they can.	Keep ball close, emphasizing touch and moving faster through the cones.
3:30-3:40	Heads-Up drill	Players dribble randomly in the penalty area and call out number of fingers coach is holding up.	Keep head up to look for passes or oncoming defenders.
3:40-3:45	Drink break	Everyone drinks 4 to 8 oz sport drink or water.	
3:45-4:00	Wind Sprints	Players run full-field sprints. Have players complete in 20 sec or less. Players jog back to start in 60 sec or less (a 3-to-1 ratio for their active recovery time).	Make sure recovery is active. Have individuals try to improve their time over the previous practice.
4:00-4:05	Drink break	Everyone drinks 4 to 8 oz sport drink or water.	

> continued

Time	Name of activity	Description	Key teaching points
4:05-4:15	2 vs. 2 scrimmages: Passing	Play 2 vs. 2: Set up multiple 15- × 20-yard grids. All players play at the same time in separate areas. Focus on passing, movement, and combination. 3 consecutive passes earn 1 point. Once the ball goes across the line, the opposing team gets the ball and begins at own end line. Play 2 min and then have teams switch grids to compete against other pairs. Allow 1 min of rest between scrimmages.	Make sure passes have a pace. Pass into space with accuracy. Work on timing the pass and the run. Freeze play when it's obvious players aren't providing passing options or reading each other.
4:15-4:30	4 vs. 4 scrimmages: Passing and tackling	Play 4 vs. 4: Set up multiple 25- × 30-yard or 35- × 40-yard grids. All players play at the same time in separate areas. Incorporate passing and tackling. Tackles in which the ball is taken directly from a player earn 2 points. Linking together three passes earns 1 point. Once the ball goes across the line, the opposing team gets the ball and begins at own end line.	Positioning for tackling: weight and stance, looking at the ball, knees slightly bent Decision making
4:30-4:35	Drink break	Everyone drinks 4 to 8 oz sport drink or water.	
4:35-4:55	8 vs. 8 game	Play game in real time, but still with modified scoring: Tackles in which possession is gained and combined with a pass earn 3 points. Combinations of 5 passes earn 1 point. Goals earn 2 points. Variation: To emphasize passing, combinations of 5 passes could earn 3 points and tackles in which possession is gained and combined with a pass could earn 1 point. If time, allow players to play without restrictions.	Offensive: Combination passing Defensive: Positioning for tackling, decision making, and maintaining possession after the tackle

Time	Name of activity	Description	Key teaching points
4:55-5:05	Cool-down and drink break	Easy jogging while dribbling; stretching. Everyone drinks 4 to 8 oz sport drink or water.	Stretch, ice, and massage any tight muscles.
5:05-5:10	Coach's comments	End-of-practice comments from the coach.	General comments; review what was learned; point out positives; announcements.

The soccer practice plan and its sample solution evaluation were developed in collaboration with Bill Schranz, former head women's soccer coach, Concordia University, Seward, Nebraska.

Practice Plan 5: Track and Field, Middle-Distance Runners

Date: March 12

Level: Varsity

Point in season: Preseason

Practice start time: 3:00 p.m.

Length of practice: 100 minutes

Practice objectives: (1) Reinforce technique skills: lifting the knees high, raising the foot directly under the butt, "pawing" the track on foot strike, avoiding overstriding, and driving the arms powerfully; (2) develop speed endurance, or the ability to run fast when tired; (3) practice concentrating on efficient running form when tired; and (4) develop the tactical skills of accelerating in the middle of a race and kicking at the end.

Equipment: Workout takes place on a 400-meter track; coach must bring stopwatches and water; runners need their racing spikes.

PRACTICE ACTIVITIES

Time	Name of activity	Description	Key teaching points
3:00-3:10	Warm-up	Easy jogging	
3:10-3:20	Warm-up	Dynamic stretching	Emphasize full range of motion in dynamic stretches.
3:20-3:30	Warm-up	5 × 100-m strides at 3/4 effort with 100-m walk recovery	Emphasize technique skills during strides.
3:30-3:35	Drink break	Everyone drinks 4 to 8 oz sport drink or water.	
3:35-4:00	Technique drills	4 × 30-m High Knee drill with 1-min recovery 4 × 30-m Butt Kick drill with 1-min recovery 4 × 30-m Fast Feet drill with 1-min recovery 4 × 1-min Arm Pumping drill with 1-min recovery	Emphasize lifting the knees to be parallel to the track. Emphasize keeping the foot close to the body and under the butt. Emphasize "pawing" action, landing with the foot moving backward. Emphasize "fast hands."
4:00-4:03	Drink break	Everyone drinks 4 to 8 oz sport drink or water.	

Time	Name of activity	Description	Key teaching points
4:03-4:23	Speed endurance interval workout	3 sets of 1 × 300 m and 1 × 200 m with 1-min recovery between the 300 and 200 and 5-min recovery between sets	For the 300s, keep the runners on 1600-m race pace. For the 200s, encourage a controlled, building sprint, adding a notch of speed every 50 m. Cue the runners to hold their form on the 200s.
4:23-4:25	Drink break	Everyone drinks 4 to 8 oz sport drink or water.	
4:25-4:35	Cool-down	10 min easy jogging	Stretch, ice, and massage any tight or sore muscles.
4:35-4:40	Coach's comments	End-of-practice comments from the coach	General comments on how the whole team practiced; recognize any outstanding efforts or performances; announcements.

Activity 6.5   Practice Plan Evaluation— *SAMPLE SOLUTIONS*

Practice Plan Evaluation: Basketball

Component	Component in plan?		If no, how could component be included?
	YES	NO	
Practice objectives are clearly stated.	X		
The format is easy to follow and contains pertinent information for each period.	X		
Practice time is used efficiently.	X		
A warm-up and stretching period is included.	X		
Ample breaks for fluid and rest are included.	X		
Periods for instruction of individual skill techniques are included.	X		
Athletes are given the opportunity to practice the techniques in gamelike conditions.	X		
Periods for instruction of individual and team tactics are included.		X	Add activity focused on individual and team tactics (e.g., Cut and Screen game) and simulate the opponent's defense. This period will provide the offensive side the opportunity to practice the individual and team tactics that are needed to make smart decisions. Review the situations with the players that determine when to flash cut, pick and roll, or cross screen. Set the standard by playing 4-on-4 where offensive players use one of the three options to gain an advantage over their defenders. After the offensive team scores 3 baskets they go on defense, the defense goes off the floor, and a new offensive group comes on. Reinforce communication among offensive team to reinforce offensive decision making that can be applied in a live game-like the 5-on-5 activity scheduled for 4:14. Consider replacing the Basic 5-on-0 activity scheduled at 4:06 or add it before this activity and extend the practice by 10 min.

Component	Component in plan?		If no, how could component be included?
	YES	NO	
Athletes are given the opportunity to practice the tactics in gamelike conditions.	X		
A cool-down period is included.	X		
A period for closing comments and announcements is included.	X		

Additional notes:

Practice Plan Evaluation: Football

Component	Component in plan?		If no, how could component be included?
	YES	NO	
Practice objectives are clearly stated.	X		
The format is easy to follow and contains pertinent information for each period.	X		
Practice time is used efficiently.	X		
A warm-up and stretching period is included.	X		
Ample breaks for fluid and rest are included.	X		
Periods for instruction of individual skill techniques are included.	X		
Athletes are given the opportunity to practice the techniques in gamelike conditions.	X		

> continued

Component	Component in plan?		If no, how could component be included?
	YES	**NO**	
Periods for instruction of individual and team tactics are included.		X	Add an activity for offensive linemen and running backs to practice the running plays that will be included in the full-team period 11-on-11 Running game, scheduled to begin at 4:18. This period will provide the offensive linemen and the running backs an opportunity to practice the individual and team tactics that are needed to run the football successfully. The new activity is called Inside Run game. A scout defense consisting of just the inside 7 will simulate the opponent's defense. The Inside Run period should be positioned before the 11-on-11 Run period.
Athletes are given the opportunity to practice the tactics in gamelike conditions.	X		
A cool-down period is included.	X		
A period for closing comments and announcements is included.	X		

Additional notes:

Practice Plan Evaluation: Volleyball

Component	Component in plan?		If no, how could component be included?
	YES	**NO**	
Practice objectives are clearly stated.	X		
The format is easy to follow and contains pertinent information for each period.	X		
Practice time is used efficiently.	X		
A warm-up and stretching period is included.	X		
Ample breaks for fluid and rest are included.	X		

Component	Component in plan?		If no, how could component be included?
	YES	NO	
Periods for instruction of individual skill techniques are included.	X		
Athletes are given the opportunity to practice the techniques in gamelike conditions.	X		
Periods for instruction of individual and team tactics are included.		X	The Weave Passing drill could be done in a shorter amount of time. Redefine that as a 10-min segment. Add a 10-min activity to the practice plan focused on individual and team tactics (e.g., Maxwell Tip drill) and simulate the opponent's defense. This activity will provide the offensive side the opportunity to practice the individual and team tactics that are needed to make smart decisions. Review the situations with the players that determine when to attack and when to tip or roll. Set the standard that in order to attack, the player must have a one-on-one situation; otherwise the player should employ the tip or roll tactic. Have defending team create one-on-one and double-blocker situations and have offensive team execute against them. Reinforce communication among offensive team to hitter's team to indicate how many blockers she is facing. This activity will reinforce offensive decision making to attack or tip/roll that will be reinforced in a live game-like 6 vs. 6 Attack or Tip/Roll practice activity scheduled for 5:03.
Athletes are given the opportunity to practice the tactics in gamelike conditions.	X		
A cool-down period is included.	X		
A period for closing comments and announcements is included.	X		

Additional notes:

Practice Plan Evaluation: Soccer

Component	Component in plan?		If no, how could component be included?
	YES	**NO**	
Practice objectives are clearly stated.	X		
The format is easy to follow and contains pertinent information for each period.	X		
Practice time is used efficiently.	X		
A warm-up and stretching period is included.	X		
Ample breaks for fluid and rest are included.	X		
Periods for instruction of individual skill techniques are included.	X		
Athletes are given the opportunity to practice the techniques in gamelike conditions.	X		
Periods for instruction of individual and team tactics are included.		X	Add a 10-min activity focused on individual and team tactics (e.g., 5 vs. 2 Keep Away). This activity will reinforce offensive decision making to make efficient, successful passes. This activity will provide the offensive side the opportunity to practice the individual and team tactics that are needed to make smart decisions. Review the situations with the players. Reinforce how players taking a step closer to receive a pass cause the defenders to react, creating distribution options for the player with the ball. Explain options if the defenders cut off passing lanes. Set the standard by starting with no touch restrictions and progress to 2 and 1 touch restrictions. Reinforce communication among offensive team to facilitate successful passes. This could replace the 2 vs. 2 activity scheduled for 4:05.
Athletes are given the opportunity to practice the tactics in gamelike conditions.	X		

Component	Component in plan?		If no, how could component be included?
	YES	NO	
A cool-down period is included.	X		
A period for closing comments and announcements is included.	X		

Additional notes:

Practice Plan Evaluation: Track and Field, Middle-Distance Runners

Component	Component in plan?		If no, how could component be included?
	YES	NO	
Practice objectives are clearly stated.	X		
The format is easy to follow and contains pertinent information for each period.	X		
Practice time is used efficiently.	X		
A warm-up and stretching period is included.	X		
Ample breaks for fluid and rest are included.	X		
Periods for instruction of individual skill techniques are included.	X		
Athletes are given the opportunity to practice the techniques in gamelike conditions.	X		
Periods for instruction of individual and team tactics are included.		X	Add a 10-min tactical period after the 4:23 drink break for middle-distance runners. Divide the runners into equal groups of 3 or 4, depending on the number of runners on the team. Select a runner to be the rabbit or front runner for each group to leave the pack, setting a fast pace early in the race. The remaining runners are to stay on a steady pace until the final lap before making their sprint to the finish line.

> continued

Practice Plan Evaluation: Track and Field, Middle-Distance Runners > *continued*

Component	Component in plan?		If no, how could component be included?
	YES	**NO**	
Athletes are given the opportunity to practice the tactics in gamelike conditions.	X		
A cool-down period is included.	X		
A period for closing comments and announcements is included.	X		

Additional notes:

Unit Summary

(Notes)

Test Preparation

Complete these steps as you prepare to take the test:

1. Read the following chapters in *Successful Coaching*:
   - Chapter 9 The Games Approach
   - Chapter 10 Teaching Technical Skills
   - Chapter 11 Teaching Tactical Skills
   - Chapter 12 Planning for Teaching
2. Complete the units related to principles of teaching in *Coaching Principles Online* component.

Coaching Successfully

1. Start developing a list of resources to determine the technical and tactical skills you should teach and how to teach them.
2. Review the resources listed in these two sections in chapter 12: Sources for Identifying Skills (covered in Step 1: Identify the Skills Your Athletes Need) and To Learn More.
3. List other tips from the instructor here.
4. Review the coach-development goals addressed in this unit and included in the table on page 101.
5. Use the space provided to briefly explain
   a. what you learned in this unit about the goals, and
   b. what you feel you should do *to improve your ability to coach successfully and help your athletes develop* by achieving these goals.
6. After the course, revisit this page and add notes that help you develop your coaching knowledge and career.

Developmental Dozen

Coach-development goals What should I do to improve my ability to coach successfully and help my athletes develop?	Athlete-development goals What athletes should achieve
4. Guide athletes to develop self-confidence: Model and teach self-confident attitudes and behaviors and create situations in which athletes experience success.	**4. Develop self-confidence.**
5. Teach the sport effectively: Teach the rules, systems, and defined plays of the sport.	**5. Learn the sport.**
6. Teach technical skills effectively: Teach correct and safe techniques.	**6. Perform technical skills well and safely.**
7. Teach sport decision-making skills effectively: Model and teach perception, attention, and concentration skills.	**7. Learn sport decision-making skills.**
8. Teach tactical skills effectively: Teach athletes how to process game situations to provide competitive advantage.	**8. Execute tactical skills well.**
9. Challenge athletes in practice and competition: Develop season and practice plans to create optimally challenging, safe, and effective practices and competitions.	**9. Strive to be better in practice and competition.**

Coaching Principles Wrap-Up

PURPOSE To help you review what you have learned in the class and understand the process and procedures for completing the rest of the Coaching Principles course.

Learning Objectives

In this unit you will learn about

- the importance of your role as a professional coach, and
- your next steps for completing the Coaching Principles course.

UNIT OVERVIEW

Topic	Activities	Time (min)
A. Coaching Is a Profession	Unit introduction Activity 7.1 Why Coaching? DVD 20 Coaching Is a Profession What coaching means to me	5
B. Next Steps	Test preparation Test procedures Coaching Successfully	5
C. Thanks and Good Luck!	Final questions Thanks and good luck!	5
TOTAL MINUTES		**15**

Coaching Is a Profession

In unit 7 we'll do a quick wrap-up of what we've covered today and review what you need to do after today to complete the Coaching Principles course.

- When we've completed this unit, you should be able to
  - describe the importance of your role as a professional coach, and
  - explain your next steps for completing the Coaching Principles course.

Activity 7.1   Why Coaching?

Instructions

1. Review your reasons for wanting to coach and the importance you placed on each reason.
2. Take a minute and consider this: Have your reasons changed in the past eight hours? Has what you think is important about coaching changed in the past eight hours?

DVD 20   Coaching Is a Profession

(Notes)

B. Next Steps

Test Preparation

1. Read all chapters in *Successful Coaching,* and read them **carefully,** because all of the test questions are based on content in the book.
2. Complete all units in *Coaching Principles Online* component. Your key code to access the online component is in the key code letter included in the Coaching Principles classroom test package. While you're in the online component, please also complete the course evaluation because your opinions are very important in helping to improve the course.

Testing

1. Review pages 1 and 2 of the Coaching Principles test instructions and determine whether you'll take the online test or the paper–pencil test.
2. Refer to page 105 in the workbook for the information you'll need to enter to start the test.

3. When you're ready to take the test, follow the instructions in the Coaching Principles test instructions.

   a. **If** you're taking the online test, follow the instructions in part B.

   b. **If** you're taking the paper–pencil test, follow the instructions in part C.

   c. You should plan to complete these two steps by _____.

   d. If you do not successfully pass your Coaching Principles test within one year of the last date of your course (today), you will have to take the entire course over again and pay all of the course fees again.

Coaching Successfully

1. Complete the Coaching Successfully activities listed at the end of units 2 through 6 in your workbook.

C. Thanks and Good Luck!

(Notes)

Test Information
Write the test information in the second column.

Required information	Write information below
Your ID number (from the course roster)	
Key code (on the top of page 1 of the Coaching Principles test instructions)	
Instructor's ID number	
Instructor's last name	
Organization code	
Last date of the course	
Course code (If you're taking the paper–pencil test, you'll need this code. The course code is located at the bottom right of the last page of the test. It begins with the letters AA followed by two numbers, for example, AA08, AA09, or AA10.)	
Date you need to complete the test by (If the instructor tells you a completion date, write it in the next column. Otherwise you should complete the test by one year from today's date; write that date in the next column.)	

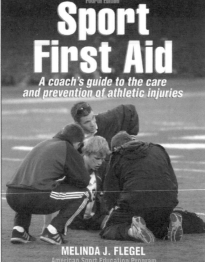